How To Be

YOUR OWN BEST PSYCHOTHERAPIST

The Key to Your Psychological Health in a Nutshell

BY

DR. MICHAEL MAMAS

Sunstar
PUBLISHING LTD.

How to Be
Your Own Best Psychotherapist
by Dr. Michael Mamas
©United States 2000
Sunstar Publishing, Ltd.
204 S. 20th Street
Fairfield, Iowa 52556

First edition 2000

Printed in the United States of America

ISBN: 1-887472-80-0

LCCN: 00-111510

Text and cover design by Irene Archer

Readers interested in obtaining further information on
the subject matter of this book are invited to corre-
spond with:

The Secretary, Sunstar Publishing, Ltd.
P.O. Box 2211, Fairfield, Iowa 52556
More Sunstar books at http://www.newagepage.com

*I would like to dedicate this book
to my students. They have filled my heart
and continue to inspire my work.*

Contents

*What is Psychological Health? Your Self-Correcting
Mechanism, Modern Psychotherapy in a Nutshell, Identity,
The Three Levels of Motivation, Exploring your Motivations,
Your Desire to Destroy, Vulnerability, Your Psychophysiological
Basenote, Exploring your Childhood Conditioning, Your
Identity With Your Conditioning, Your Relationship With,
Non-attachment vs. "Letting Go," Your First and Second
Responses, First and Second Responses in Your Personal
Relationships*

Transference, The Five Divine Currents

Acknowledgments

There are so many people who have dedicated their time and effort to assisting me in bringing out this knowledge. I feel I can never thank them enough or fully convey to them my appreciation.

I would like to thank my wife, Tanja, for her love and her unending dedication and support of this work. Thanks to my daughter, Jaya, for the purity of her love and enduring innocence while I spent hours at the computer instead of with her, playing outside or on our living room floor.

With respect to this book, I would like to thank Bonnie Rost and Clif Liu for the many hours they devoted to this project. I would also like to thank Betty Hottel for her unending dedication and support. Thanks to Arthur Cook for his selfless commitment and tireless service. Thanks to Dr. David Cornsweet for his insights, expertise, and commitment. Thanks to Gregg Lein for his many years of guidance. Thanks to Mark Putnam for his dedication to bringing out this knowledge. Thanks to Marion and Billy Benge for their advice and vision.

But I would like to thank them all mostly for the love and friendship they have given and continue to give to me, my wife, and our daughter. It is a great honor and privilege to have each one of you as my friend and confidante.

Foreword

The art of psychotherapy is about to take an evolution-
ary step forward. In this little book, Dr. Michael
Mamas proposes a radically different yet profoundly simple approach to the process of self-actualization. This
powerful understanding of the human condition has
helped many lead deeper, more fulfilling lives. This
approach, which Dr. Mamas has termed *Transgradient
Counseling*™, has an incredibly powerful potential to help
us gain deeper and deeper levels of self-knowledge.

Since working with the principles of *Transgradient
Counseling* over the past six years, I've watched my clients
move faster and deeper in therapy than I ever thought possible. Those suffering from depression feel better quicker,
relationship issues untangle, and those who just feel stagnant
in their lives resolve their dilemma and move on quickly. I
sit in awe as a participant in my clients' unfoldment.

A quick note to my fellow professionals: We have
invested a lot of time, energy, and money in our training.
We mean well and pride ourselves in our ability to help and
"be with" our clients. Much of what Dr. Mamas presents
can be threatening. It may be tempting to dismiss it with,
"Oh sure, I get it." Please don't do yourself this disservice.
Take the time to explore your relationship with your mod-

els and preconceived notions. Challenge yourself to loosen your beliefs on what you believe your clients should think or feel in any given situation. See what happens when you risk knowing nothing. Sit with your clients as they explore their inner landscape from a multitude of perspectives. Join in that exploration with them. I can promise you that you will become a better therapist. I have seen the impact this work has had on those professionals who have studied with Dr. Mamas. You will free yourself from the onerous burden of always having to be one step ahead of your client. You will develop a deeper respect and appreciation for those who enter your office. Remember, psycho means "soul" in Greek; *theraputae* means "healer." Take the risk of exploring your models, beliefs, and self to become a true facilitator of the healing of souls.

David Cornsweet, Ph.D., D.A.P.A.
Certified Diplomate in Psychotherapy
September 12, 2000

Dr. David Cornsweet is a licensed psychotherapist in private practice, and a certified diplomate of the American Psychotherapy Association. He has over thirty years of experience in the field, and has studied with many of the acknowledged masters of psychology in both western and eastern traditions. Dr. Cornsweet is regarded widely as an innovator in mind/body integration. He has taught in numerous schools and training programs throughout the country. Currently, Dr. Cornsweet resides in Del Mar, California with his wife, Jennifer, and his son, Daniel.

Introduction

This book, a transcription of a four-day lecture series I recently gave in New York City, is not just about theory. It is a tour through your inner landscape that concludes with a healthier, wiser, and happier you. Each section corresponds with one day of the training. At the end of some of the chapters are questions. I suggest that as you go through the book, you write down your answers to these questions in a separate notebook, and refer back to them when you are asked to do so.

Why You Must Be
Your Own Best Psychotherapist

What does it mean to be psychologically healthy?

The experts disagree. According to a recent count, there are over two hundred and fifty distinct types of psychotherapy. That doesn't include spiritual and holistic approaches.

Therapeutic methods vary widely. Some therapists hypnotize you, others try to program (or deprogram) you. Some tell you how to behave, others tell you how to misbehave. Some think it is their job to figure you out, others hold you under a mattress and tell you to fight your way out.

As a group, psychotherapists have not come to any consensus of what it means to be psychologically healthy or how to help their clients attain psychological health. Consequently, unless you wish to cast your fate to the wind, you must take charge of your own psychotherapy and look to the fundamentals. Only then do the divergent perspectives come together and make sense. Not only *can* you be your own best psychotherapist, you *must* be. The alternative is to play dice with your own mental health.

There is an additional and very important reason why

you must become your own best psychotherapist: to live life responsibly. This requires that you be psychologically healthy. The alternative is to live your life as a victim of your own psychological conditionings and traumas. It is of utmost importance that you spend some time exploring and working with the landscape of your inner psyche. In our culture we understand that if you do not brush your teeth, your health will suffer. Likewise, if you do not "brush the teeth of your own psychological landscape," your life will suffer.

In my years of teaching advanced training programs, I have come across a small handful of psychotherapists who I feel have a solid and responsible approach to helping their clients. It has been fascinating for me to note that every single one of them say the same thing about their work. They essentially say, "I have rejected much of what I learned from my psychotherapeutic training. Of course I picked up a little here and there that was of value and incorporate it, but I certainly don't practice what I was taught. I don't understand what I do, I only know that it works." After attending my lectures and workshops, they tell me that what I am offering is not only a clear understanding, but a systematic practical approach to their work. They feel it is where psychotherapy has been trying to go since its inception, and call it the next major step in the field of psychotherapy.

I do not call what I teach psychotherapy. I call it *Transgradient Counseling*™. Some classify my work as spiritual counseling. Though I am uncomfortable with some of the connotations that title carries, I am willing to be put into that category. It is not to be employed as an approach that is suitable for the mentally or emotionally unstable, but is directed more to people of reasonable stability and psychological health. Yet, I believe its underlying principles are fundamental to everyone and all of life. Whether you choose to work with a psychotherapist or not, I feel you will find these principles to be invaluable in understanding yourself and others. Literally thousands of people have benefited from this practical knowledge.

In my years of private practice, a large percentage of my clientele became composed of psychotherapists who learned about me through their clients and decided they wanted to work with me themselves. One psychotherapist who happened to know a number of my students once said, "I have only one question for you. Where do you find all of those incredible people?" I responded by saying, "Everyone is already incredible. I only introduce people to who it is they truly are."

Chapter 1

Day One:
Understanding the Human Psyche

L osing yourself to the complexity of your life is like losing the landscape of the forest to the details of a tree.
You can navigate the waters of your most complex problem
by understanding a few fundamental principles. Today we
are going to explore those principles. They are the gateway to a healthier, happier, and more productive you.

What is Psychological Health?

Our psychological health is really just a matter of stress. But I mean the word "stress" in a larger sense than what you feel at the end of a busy day. By "stress," I mean any fatigue or distortion imposed upon our physiology that impacts our psychological health. I refer to that part of the physiology as the psychophysiology. Just as we have a physiology that determines our physical health, we have a psychophysiology that determines our psychological health.

There is a very direct and intimate connection between the amount of stress that we have accumulated in our psychophysiology and the state of our psychological health. For example, if we have a particularly jolting experience, such as an emotional trauma, it has a physiological correlate. If that trauma impacts the physiology significantly enough, it is held in the psyche as a distortion, or stress. Stress can result from an occurrence that is experienced as either negative or positive.

Your Self-Correcting Mechanism

The development of psychodynamic health (the healthy function of the psychophysiology) has to do with the alleviation of stress. Inherent in that statement is a rather intriguing understanding: the state of the physiology itself is intrinsic to the state of psychodynamic health. I don't think modern psychotherapy embraces this understanding to the extent to which it should. This understanding is fundamental to an effective, wise, and intelligent approach to psychological health. I sometimes express it by saying, "You're already fine. It's just the stress in the physiology that needs to be purified out. The basis of your psychodynamic health, inner wisdom, and intelligence is already there."

We know that if we cut our finger all we have to do is put a bandage on it and keep it clean. The inner intelligence, an inner self-correcting mechanism, will cause it to grow back together. The finger knows how to grow back together. We just have to create a situation that accommodates that process.

We need to recognize that the self-correcting mechanism which heals our finger is the same mechanism that comes into play in our psychological health. Our attitude about our mental health is that we need to impose health upon it from the outside. We say, "Think this way. Hold on to these commandments. Get rid of that aspect of your being. Align with this behavioral modality. Do it like this and you will be healthy." If you look at the modern approach to psychotherapy, that is generally what you see.

Everyone knows that a rose bud cannot be turned into a blossom by peeling back the petals. Doing that would only make a mess out of the bud. Everyone knows the ability of the bud to unfold into an exquisite blossom is inherent in the nature of the plant. Our psychological health is the same. I call that inner intelligence the self-correcting mechanism.

Modern Psychotherapy in a Nutshell

Modern psychotherapy can be understood as consisting of three different fundamental approaches. In practice, most modern psychotherapeutic approaches are a combination of the three.

The first is the cognitive approach. In this approach you develop some intellectual understanding of what's going on in your head. Maybe you have issues with your mother. Or maybe you have issues with men. The idea is that because you have a cognitive understanding (you understand intellectually what you have been doing wrong), the next time you meet a man, you decide that you won't act in your habitual way. But to draw a parallel to the finger, the cut is still there. It hasn't grown together—it's not healed. There is no organic physiological change in your psyche that has taken place as a result of the cognitive approach. You are just holding on to a new attitude, an overlay. You may say to yourself, "Okay, now I get what I was doing, so now I'm going to do this instead." But all the organic physiological attributes that were there before still remain.

The second approach is the behavioral approach. By modifying your behavior you attempt to change your psyche. For example, suppose you want to be successful in life. The therapist might prescribe a program like this: on the first day, before you go to bed, you write down everything that you want to accomplish tomorrow. On the second day, you force yourself to do at least three things that are on your list. This approach is like jumping through hoops. Each day you jump through a new hoop and in thirty days you'll be a "new you." Like the cognitive approach, there's no organic physiological change that takes place in you. You have only overlaid a modified behavior.

The third aspect of modern psychotherapy is the affective approach—emotional release. If you feel angry towards somebody, the therapist tells you to pretend that the pillow on the floor is that person, and encourages you to beat it up. There can be some organic change here, but it's manipulation. You're pushing the physiology in a certain direction you are told it should go. You're forcing something out. Often more distortion is driven into the psychophysiology than is released, if any is released at all. In contrast, when we heal the cut finger, all we do is accommodate the innate self-correcting mechanism. The finger knows how to heal. We don't grab the skin, force it together, and try to make it grow according to our guidelines. We know that it will grow together on its own.

So this idea of the self-correcting mechanism, as it applies to the human psyche, is really revolutionary. It is not the way psychotherapy is usually understood to work. We usually try to make our psyche function in some manner that we think is better. A psychotherapist might think, "Well, I see this is going on with my client's psyche, and if I can get him to stop functioning that way and start functioning this other way, then he'll be healthy." It's what I call out/in. You look at the surface of your client, and you try to drive your ideas into his depth. You have some parameters or convictions about what a person would be like on the surface if he or she was healthy. Based on that ideal, you gauge your client's level of health and try to restructure whatever you can identify and access on the surface of his or her being. Once your client starts lining up with your ideas, you declare your client's inner being to be healthy. That's out/in. Starting from the outer and trying to work into the inner. It has nothing to do with the self-correcting mechanism.

I compare the out/in approach to building a 25-story structure starting with the 25th floor. You use props and scaffolding to hold it up. Next you build the 24th floor under it, employing more props and scaffolding. Then you put in the 23rd floor along with more props, and so on. Eventually, you work your way down to the foundation. But there is going to be some misalignment. There has to be.

Likewise, when you apply the out/in approach to your psyche, things are not going to align with the depth of your own inner being. The out/in approach does not respect the uniqueness at the depth of your inner being. It's all about the surface.

The in/out approach, on the other hand, recognizes your innate wisdom. Just as your finger heals with an innate intelligence, so does your psychodynamic structure. If you just allow that intelligence to be the guiding light and the determining factor that facilitates the healing, then you're working in a way that's in accord with your nature. You are tapping into that place in the depth of your being that is already fine, has always been fine, and always will be fine; and just allowing the rest of your psyche to align with it. It is something that is inaccessible, and cannot be defined from any superficial perspective of what you are supposed to be like. It honors the freedom and naturalness necessary to accommodate the uniqueness of your own individuality.

Question: Isn't the self-correcting mechanism somehow accessed by the traditional approach of psychotherapy?

The self-correcting mechanism is initiated by the out/in approach to some extent. But the problem is that it is an accidental side effect. It may happen, but the entire focus of our own whole personal psychodynamic process needs to be founded upon that understanding. To depend on just an occasional accidental side effect is not effective therapy. Staying focused on the facilitation (or awakening or freeing) of the self-correcting mechanism is the most important thing.

Identity

We already mentioned that improving psychological health is about alleviating stress. What is stress? What form does it take? What's its nature? How does it look or act when it impacts the human psychology? And how can we facilitate the self-correcting mechanism?

The first way stress impacts the human psyche is through what I call identity. We "identify with" things. It's as if the physiology gets programmed when it is impacted with stress. In other words, it gets conditioned. This conditioning can take the form of your affinities as well as your aversions.

Each of us has developed a habitual identity with different modes of behavior that are more a functioning of our conditioning than the functioning of our true nature. One behavioral example might be smoking. We condition the physiology to desire something that's killing us. Another example might be our relationship with men: "All men are jerks." Another example might be our relationship with women: "All women are stupid." Another example might be our belief systems about the world: "It's not safe to go out there. It's a dangerous place." These are some examples of aversions.

Another common aversion is a dislike of the intellect: "Oh, I don't want to think, I just want to feel." Others have aversions to emotions: "Emotions are a waste of time." That is a form of denial. We feel things, but we want to deal with life by being like Mr. Spock or Commander Data from Star Trek. What we are trying to do is wall off aspects of our being. It doesn't work.

Conditioning can also be the basis of your affinities. Some of these affinities are so sweet and so innocent that you might ask, "Well, how can that be wrong?" I remember I was giving a lecture and mentioned what I call the "love and light" mentality: going through life trying to view everything with love and thinking, "Oh, we're all love and it's all beautiful. We all have to just see the sunny side of people and life." A lady at that lecture (she was very sweet really) put up her hand and said, "Well, you know, you're saying that about being loving and all, but how can that be bad?" And she said it from such a sincere, innocent, and loving place, that it really touched my heart. "How can that be bad? Wouldn't it be wonderful if we had a world where everybody loved each other? Maybe if we all started living that now it would make the world a better place." But there are other realities, other aspects of life that we need to allow for. Why? Because it is simply the nature of life. Otherwise, you're going to walk down the street in love and light, and get mugged. So affinities based upon stress, even our most laudable and noble affinities, ultimately get in our way, as do our stress-based aversions.

So our evolution is about resting into that value of our being that is already fine, that's already healthy and integrated, that spontaneously and naturally upholds all aspects of our life. And that has to come from in/out, just as much as the healing of a cut on our finger has to come from in/out, not out/in. So the wisdom of facilitating our own personal process parallels the same simple and obvious wisdom we have about healing our cut finger. What is truly amazing is that our society has embraced an approach to mental health that has lost sight of this simple truth.

Yes, there are things we can do to facilitate that process, but they must be done with a certain humility. This humility comes from the understanding that healing cannot be done by aligning with some superficial identification of how it is we think someone is supposed to be. Although different psychological concepts and notions can be useful, they can hinder you if your relationship with them isn't healthy. To be healthy, that relationship needs to be based upon an in/out approach.

Although these different psychological understandings must not be used to create a system or set of buzzwords with which to align your psyche, they may have a function. They can be used to "till the soil," or to free up our psychophysiology, so that we then naturally rest into the intrinsic, already healthy, and already fine value at the basis of our being. In other words, we can use them to loosen the stress and purify it out of our physiology. When the stress has been purified out, you discover that you are fine. You've always been fine. It's just that all the stresses that have been imposed upon you and taken the form of your identities have gotten in your way.

Questions To Facilitate Your Inner Exploration

If you would like, I recommend that you get a notebook and write down your answers to the questions at the end of these chapters. We will work with your answers as you go through this book.

1. What are some of your attributes that you feel particularly good about?

2. What are some of your attributes that you would like to change?

3. Make a list of people that you respect, admire, or have an affinity for. Make a list of their positive attributes that you appreciate.

4. Make a list of people that you have an aversion toward. Include a list of their attributes that you do not care for.

The Three Levels of Motivation

How do we responsibly do our personal process? We'll start with some principles. The first principle is the notion of motivation. It's a very important term. Motivation, we could say, exists on three levels.

Motivation of Communion

At the source of your being, your motivations are based upon that place inside that's already fine, that's pure. In that place, your motivations involving your relationships with other people are quite laudable. They are to perpetuate the feeling of communion in love, to make things better, and to be in support of all concerned. It's a very positive and life-supporting sort of motivation that's inherent to your own true nature. Your own true nature is pure. Every individual's essential underlying nature is pure. From that pure place at the basis of our being, what motivates us is the desire to share that purity with others.

Subconscious Motivation

At the depth of even the most wicked person is loving, compassionate, and pure intent. What they do may be totally inexcusable, but at the depth of even a murderer's being is purity. What happens is that as stress accumulates in the physiology, the psyche gets distorted. Little kids don't care about belief systems, models, or identities. All they care about is Mommy's and Daddy's love. They just want to feel loved. If Mommy says, "You're bad if you do this," they try not to do it. When Mommy says, "You're good," they feel her love. This is where the overlays start to take root. Children begin to identify with whatever behavioral modality seems to get them what they long for: communion and love. Over time, the purity of that underlying motivation becomes shrouded underneath the distortions resulting from these identity overlays.

In our workings on a day to day level, these distortions result in a second level of motivation; yet it is often hidden in our subconscious mind. Getting in touch with your hidden motivations is a major part of tilling the soil of your own inner landscape. It is very much about self-honesty. The motivation behind what you do or what you say can be very elusive at times.

Conscious Motivation

The third level of motivation is the most superficial. It's the motivation that we're clear about and comfortable with in our conscious awareness. We believe and tell ourselves and others that it's our real motivation. You can say to somebody, "I love you," and believe you are being honest and straightforward. But you can simultaneously have a hidden underlying motivation that says, "I hate you," that it is actually based on: "I hate you because you don't love me, so I want to make you feel bad by telling you that I love you." But it is not stated or even understood. Where you think your motivation comes from is actually only the surface. Of course, simultaneously, you have the underlying pure motivation based in the longing for communion, love, and mutual support. However, this deepest purest love is usually hidden from view, buried under the stress in the psychophysiology that creates our more superficial and distorted motivations.

Questions To Facilitate Your Inner Exploration

1. Think of a recent conflict you had with someone, and remember the things you said to that person.

2. What did you tell yourself your motivation was for saying those things?

3. Can you identify a more hidden motivation that was making a very different statement or had a different

intent than what you told them, as well as yourself?

4. Look even more deeply to identify a place within you
    that had a deeper longing that lay at the very basis of
    this interaction (the place where you long for the puri-
    ty of communion and mutual appreciation with that
    person).

Exploring Your Motivations

Examining our motivation can be a very powerful tool
to facilitate the exploration of our inner psyche. It is exploration that tills the soil and frees up the psychophysiology,
so that it can begin to self-correct and thereby function
from that place of underlying harmony, intelligence, and
wisdom. That place dwells at the depth of not only our
physical being that heals a cut, but also our personality
being that heals our psyche, if only we allow it to happen.
But if we hang on to the surface justifications, (for example, "I love you") and if we're not in touch with the underlying statement that says, "I hate you because you don't
love me," the underlying convolutions and twists become
frozen. We lose touch with what lies at that deeper and
more altruistic level that is consistent with our own inner
purity.

The underlying motivation behind every action is to
commune with something; for example, a person, knowledge, or an ideal. It's all about bringing things together to
greater and greater levels of fullness and wholeness with-

in our psyche and life. But as this motivation to commune
wells up to the two more superficial levels of motivation,
it can get quite distorted. One level may not be talking
honestly to the others. The real quest is to start to use this
notion of motivation as a means to explore your own inner
landscape. What are the three levels of motivation? They
are the pure motivation of communion, the intermediate
subconscious hidden motivation, and the superficial conscious motivation behind the things you say and do.

Remember that the deepest level of motivation always
has to do with communion. Bringing separation back to
oneness. That's the deepest level of motivation, and it
underlies all the levels of your being. So the deepest,
purest motivation behind all of our actions is communion,
to bring separation back to oneness.

Your Desire to Destroy

The three levels of motivation are always connected
to one another, even though that connection can go
through snarls, tangles, and twangs as it works its way
from one level to the next. You cannot understand another person if you cannot see that within them the deepest
underlying motivation is always the longing to take separation and bring it to oneness. The crudest attempt for
oneness is through annihilation. If you don't feel one with
something, and you want to feel your oneness, just destroy
or consume it. I once watched a Saturday morning car-
toon about the animal that twirls around like a top. He

was spinning around and appeared in front of some other animal, ready to devour it. A little commentary voice said, "Prepare for the bonding experience of a lifetime!" Animals, when they devour, unify with. They become one with, they bond with what it is they destroy. So through destruction we feel that we unify, but it can be a very twisted form of unification. A racist feels hatred toward those who aren't like him. The twisted impulse is that the best way to feel unity with everything out there is to simply destroy that which feels foreign. Then you are left feeling oneness with everything that is. The underlying impetus is for unity, oneness with everything that is.

Does the longing for union lie at the basis of all our actions? It's the impetus of why you got up this morning. It's the underlying motivation that propels all of life. It's even why you're sitting there right now: to create deeper and deeper levels of communion. The motivation is to unify with that with which you don't feel fully connected, or don't understand. And it's not over-standing. It is under-standing. There's humility and purity built right into the name: understanding. That brings up the next concept: the notion of vulnerability.

Vulnerability

As human beings, we are all incredibly vulnerable creatures. So getting in touch with our own vulnerability is another powerful tool we can use in the tilling of the soil of our psyche. If we feel weak, we become hard on the surface in an attempt to defend ourselves. This is directly proportional to the degree of frailty that we feel inside. For example, suppose you see some big tough guy walking down the street with an aggressive attitude. What you are really seeing is an incredibly vulnerable creature that finds his vulnerability so unbearable, for whatever reason, that he presents a very hard and powerful surface.

Can we sense a person's inner landscape? Yes. We are caricatures of our inner landscape. I like to say it like this: we think we hide, but we don't. We wear everything about ourselves right on the surface. As you begin to explore your own inner landscape, what are you really exploring? You are exploring humanity. And as you get more and more in touch with your own humanity, you start to discover that your humanity is common to all of humanity. So as you understand your own inner landscape, you very instinctively, without having to study it, understand the people around you. It's very beautiful. We are all incredibly vulnerable creatures. We may all be doing our own unique dances, but we're all in the same playroom, playing with the same toys.

Question: Is the longing to commune based in our fear of being alone?

It's a beautiful question. What does this longing for oneness really have its basis in? Is it based in fear? It is not based in fear. It's based in love, the opposite of fear. We long to commune because it's our inherent nature, at the depth of our being, to love.

Our fear is what prevents us from functioning from that place. We may fear that if we show our vulnerability, we'll look like a fool. So we create a facade, an overlay. But as the psyche heals, we integrate all the different levels of our being so that we function harmoniously with our vulnerability in a fulfilling manner that is unique to each individual. Then our vulnerability naturally interfaces with what's occurring on the surface of our life.

So there is an intelligence built into our nature that needs to be freed up to function coherently so we can show our vulnerability in a responsible manner. Otherwise, our vulnerability and fear can compel us to collapse into a hopeless pile of protoplasm. Our fear is based on a lack of integration between our different parts. In fear, the different aspects of our being do not function harmoniously. We sense that hidden inside, there's some aspect of our self that is not "talking to" the other aspects. In other words, when we know, deep down, that we're not playing with a full deck, we tighten up and feel afraid. What keeps us from playing with a full deck? Stress, which shows through our identities.

So stress in the physiology is the basis of fear. And I'm talking about fear in a physiologically conditioned sense. I'm not saying that if someone points a gun at you, you shouldn't feel any fear. That's a different kind of fear. I'm talking about the fear that has its basis in your stress, independent of external influences. It's something you fall into regularly just based on the unbalanced state of the psychophysiology. That brings up another notion: the psychophysiological base note.

Your Psychophysiological Base Note

When we are put under pressure, we buckle in a certain way that depends on the nature of the stresses in our physiology. We buckle into what I call our psychophysiological base note. It is like the weakest link in a chain. For one person it may be anger. Every day something happens that makes her angry. Another person may feel sad all the time. He thinks to himself, "Oh, I watched the news, and it made me feel so sad." His psychophysiological base note is sadness. What are some other common psychophysiological base notes? Where do you go when your physiology is under strain? Fear is a major one. Frustration can be one also. We usually have one primary psychophysiological base note that keeps coming up, but the system can collapse into different secondary base notes like greed or hunger. Not hunger in the sense of food, but rather hunger in the sense of wanting, neediness, and pride.

Even our psychophysiological base notes can have hidden agendas attached to them. So when we feel stress, we might kick into laughter. How many people you know laugh or smile when they go into fear? This is one of many examples of various possible convolutions of the physiological landscape. The important question is what are *your* convolutions? In other words, what is the nature of *your* inner landscape?

Sometimes you can show anger when you're afraid. Sometimes you can show fear when you are angry. Sometimes we go into confusion and helplessness. How could confusion be a good defense? Suppose you grew up in a family of scientists that pounded away at you with their intellects when you were a child. As they pounded away, you didn't have the vocabulary to debate with them. Yet there was an inner part of your being that knew better; you just couldn't give expression to it intellectually. You couldn't go toe to toe with your parents. Where would your psyche buckle? It could buckle down into confusion. That ongoing childhood situation could create your psychophysiological base note. So even as an adult, when you undergo stress or pressure, you would often experience confusion.

Questions To Facilitate Your Inner Exploration

1. What is your psychophysiological base note?

2. What are some examples, from your recent past, when you went into your psychophysiological base note?

3. Do you use it as a defense in some way?

Exploring Your Childhood Conditioning

This brings up another important subject: childhood conditioning. The pure vessel of our physiology gets conditioned based on the interactions we have in childhood.

So an excellent tool to access our inner psychodynamic landscape is exploring our childhood. The exploration involves asking questions like:

What were your childhood relationships like?
What was your relationship with your mother like?
What was your relationship with your father like?
What was their relationship with each other like when you were growing up?
What was the relationship like between your brothers, sisters, and you?
How did you fit into the whole family circle as a child?
What was your role in your family?
What psychophysiological base note did you "buckle into" in those situations?
Where did you go emotionally?
How did you deal with it?
How did you deal with your motivations when you were a kid?

Notice that in our explorations, we are beginning to combine the concepts that we have introduced: psychophysiological base note, childhood, and motivation. I would like to encourage you to combine everything that you learn here as you do your inner exploration.

As children, we all go through many emotions in our relationships. It is important to remember them and feel them again as part of our inner exploration. Then our childhood becomes the gateway into exploring our inner landscape as an adult. Our childhood is like a little universe that projects out on to the whole of our adult life.

Exploring your childhood is a fundamental part of your psychophysiological healing. Behavioral patterns and identities get created in childhood. If you can bring those childhood patterns to light, you'll gain a tremendous amount of healing and insight into what you do and how you function. Your habits formed around how you compromised yourself to get Mommy's and Daddy's love. As a kid, you didn't mind compromising yourself because you didn't have a belief system, an identity you held with a death's grip (I call it white knuckling). You have carried your childhood identities, formed in the innocence of your relationship with your parents, forward into your adult life.

Questions To Facilitate Your Inner Exploration

1. What was your childhood like? Give a brief history. Tell the story, but more importantly, remember the feelings associated with those times and experiences.

2. What was the relationship between your mother and father like while your mother was pregnant with you?

3. What do you know about your birth? Was it easy or difficult?

4. What was your relationship with your mother like when you were an infant? Was she attentive? Was she

preoccupied with other things? You can ask people you know about this. Alternatively, you can explore how you feel things must have been for you as an infant.

5. What was your relationship with each of your parents like before you started school? When you were in elementary school? Junior High? High School? What was your relationship like with them in your twenties, thirties, etc.?

6. What has your relationships with your brothers and/or sisters been like throughout your life? How were your parents involved in those relationships?

7. What were your early experiences of dating and sex like?

8. Discuss any occurrences in your childhood that seemed to have a particular impact on you.

Remember these experiences do not define you. Exploring these questions helps till the soil of your being so the self-correcting mechanism can do its work.

Your Identity With Your Conditioning

Often we create some sort of idealized notion of what we will be like when we are self-improved. We invest our whole lifetime into conforming to these idealized notions, but in the end all we've done is reinforced another level of overlay in the name of self-improvement. It actually annihilates us. We get buried so far beneath these conditionings that we become identified with them. We don't know who we really are anymore. We succeed in convincing ourselves that we are the conditionings.

You probably know of psychotherapists or self-help gurus that are buried in their idealized notions. On the surface they seem so together. But there's a part of you that doesn't quite believe it. You may have the urge to cry, "Snap out of it and talk to me!" But they would not hear you; they might just say, "I am talking to you." They are so lost in their overlays that they think that is who they are. Many people who have traveled the self-help path for a long time end up this way. They apply a little Band-Aid over one aspect of their being they don't like, then another little Band-Aid over some other aspect, and then another. After 30 years of applying Band-Aids, they're covered and you can't get through to them. It's sad because they think they know all about self-improvement. They think they have all the answers and have it all together. The truth is, their relationship with their innate being has been lost.

Questions To Facilitate Your Inner Exploration

1. Think of people you know who you feel are identified with a conditioning (an overlay). How can you tell they are identified with an overlay? How does it make you feel? What would you like to say to them if you feel they could receive it?

2. How might you be identified with a conditioning? How does it affect your life? What comes up within you if you consider letting go of that conditioning?

Your Relationship With . . .

So it's critical to create a healthy relationship with yourself. It's not so much about getting rid of the conditionings or aspects of yourself that you do not like, such as anger, as having a healthy relationship with them. How deeply is your anger impregnated into your being? Is it a result of stress in the physiology or is it just a facet of your nature?

Your anger is not the problem. Your relationship with your anger is what needs to be explored. If you try to get rid of your anger, you're just trying to turn yourself into an automaton, a machine attempting to align with some idealized notion of a healthy and evolved person. You'll never live up to it because it's out/in. It's trying to turn an apple into an orange.

Really understanding that you are already fine deep inside is extremely important. Healing is just a matter of resting into your own fineness, not trying to program your head, your emotions, your heart, and everything else to function in accord with some model you have bought into. If you spend years programming yourself and get really good at conforming to an idealized notion, all you've got to show for it at the end of your life is so much Band-Aid therapy that you are Teflon-coated. It's not you.

Exploring your "relationship with" various aspects of

your being is what clears the stress and triggers the self-correcting mechanism. Then your relationship with these aspects of yourself shifts in a manner that is consistent with your inner nature. Hoping that your anger will go away and never appear again is asking too much of yourself. Developing a healthier relationship with your anger is a very realistic alternative.

Of course, life is not about aligning with some idealized notion! It's about discovering who you are—your own uniqueness. If there's such a thing as grace, divine grace, it is that you are already fine! What could possibly be a more graceful universe than one in which we are all already fine at the root of our being? Our only task is to let ourselves be who we are.

So how do you know when something is a Band-Aid or when it's your own true nature? Life is subtle and tricky. You don't always know. But you can feel your way. Sometimes it's blatantly obvious. For example, in your exploration of your childhood, a light bulb in your head may go off: "Oh my God, I got that from my mother, and I really don't think that. That's just what my mother kept saying." Sometimes it is subtle and difficult to fathom fully. But the good news is you don't have to know if it's a Band-Aid or your true nature. All you need to do is continue to explore and reflect. Life is not black and white. It is elusive and subtle. That is a part of life's beauty.

Unfortunately, what commonly happens in psychotherapy is that we explore and till the soil only to come to a conclusion: "Oh, now I get it. I've been doing this, so I'm just going to stop doing that, and start doing this other thing." That conclusion just leads to another overlay. So if you ever conclude that one perspective is a Band-Aid and the other is "my truth," and reject one while grasping the other, you're creating another Band-Aid. It's very subtle. It's the exploration that awakens the self-correcting mechanism. All of the codes of ethics, behavioral models, self-help tools, and psychological notions are only of value to facilitate the exploration. They're not the gold. They're the pick axes and shovels of your own inner exploration. Your inner nature is the gold! That understanding makes a huge difference. As soon as you decide that the shovel is the gold, you abandon the self and align with an overlay.

Questions To Facilitate Your Inner Exploration

1. Recall the list you made of your undesirable attributes. Go through them one at a time and explore your relationship with them. Do they make you judge yourself? Do you beat yourself up over them? Do you try to force yourself to overcome them? Do you feel you are too apathetic toward them? Do you wish you could surgically remove them from your being?

2. How might your "relationship with" those attributes shift as it becomes healthier?

3. What is your "relationship with" your answers to ques-

tion #2 above? Do they make you judge yourself? Do you beat yourself up, etc.? Are you trying to conform to an idealized notion of a healthier relationship with these attributes? Remember, the exploration is the healing.

For example, if one is your anger, how do you feel toward yourself after you have gotten angry? How did you learn to feel that way about your anger? Can you remember similar situations from childhood? If so, what were your parents' attitudes toward your anger? Have you internalized their attitudes? Can you think of other attitudes toward your anger that may be constructive to explore? Remember, this is not about finding "the right attitude" to hold on to. It is just an exploration. The exploration is what facilitates the healing. It's not about creating a new overlay to identify with so you can either sweep your anger under the rug or "wear your anger on your shoulder." It is not about deciding that you get it now and the exploration is finished. The exploration never ends. A healthy relationship with life is an unending exploration.

Non-attachment Versus "Letting Go"

Does this notion of our relationship with the overlay relate to the idea of attachment and non-attachment? It's all about attachment and non-attachment, but we can get attached to being nonattached. The notion of white knuckling versus letting go (attachment verses non-attachment) has been misunderstood throughout the ages. There are entire religious orders, in the East as well as the

West, that think non-attachment implies some form of renunciation of worldly life. "Oh, I'm beyond identity and want to live a spiritual life. I'm going to give away all of my money, forsake the family and nice clothes, and live the life of a monk." That's not at all what we're talking about here. That perspective of renunciation is a fundamental misunderstanding of the fine fabric that underlies our psyche and is fundamental to mental health.

To understand mental health we first have to understand the nature of what it means to be human, what life is, and what existence is. Otherwise, there's no context for the study. If you don't have the proper context, an idea, notion, and principle here and there are just little fragments. They're a set of disconnected ideas.

The problem with the notion of non-attachment is so many people have gotten attached to it. It ends up being attachment to non-attachment. So they walk around doing non-attachment and saying, "Oh, I'm not attached to anything. I'm beyond identity." And that's called one big huge identity with the notion of non-attachment. So non-attachment isn't about how your outer life looks. You can be abundantly wealthy and love ice cream, and really enjoy your new car, while still living the true meaning of non-attachment. True non-attachment is a state of psychophysiological freedom. It means a freedom that is not frozen and programmed with overlays and identities. Non-attachment means resting into your own inner nature.

How do we know if we are living our own true nature? We hold this stuff lightly. It's the nature of life. The beauty of it is we don't have to know, nature knows. Our own nature knows that we're already fine. It's not our job to figure it out. It's our job to till the soil, so we spontaneously function from our own intrinsic nature, which turns out to be wonderful. You're already fine.

So practically speaking, when something challenging comes up in life, how do we deal with it? This question brings up the next major point, the concept of the first and second response.

Your First and Second Responses

Imagine that you're angry. You feel it with all of your being. Every fiber of your being says you want to lash out. This expression of anger is justified in some self-help and New Age circles with, "This is my truth. I'm speaking my truth."

Your truth is not something that lives on the surface of your being. Your truth lies quietly at the depth of your being. It is your eternal quest in the name of your own self-unfoldment and psychodynamic health to pursue your truth. Like the pursuit of the silver chalice, you'll never grab on to your truth, but the eternal quest for it brings you to greater and greater levels of mental health. So I've talked about the first response: your gut level knee-jerk reaction.

Your second response is something that you come to through reflection, pondering, questioning, thinking, waiting, feeling, and perhaps coming back into balance. Then the idea is to come up with, not *the* second response, but *a* second response. And not something that you decide, "Oh okay, I looked at this for 15 minutes or 2 days, and now I know my second response." You found a truth (not the one ultimate truth) that lies deeper than your knee-jerk conditioning.

Question: But sometimes I just can't help it. I go with my first response.

That speaks to the nature of conditioning, and what I call the sticky nature of existence. It's easy to get stuck. This stuff is programmed into our physiology. Maybe we know better, but we just can't help it. Life is better viewed not as a test, but as an exploration. We work with these things. We don't judge ourselves by them. As stress purifies out, our first response more and more comes into harmony with our second response. As we purify the stress out of our physiology, our first response becomes more in balance. In any given moment, anybody can have an inappropriate first response, but as stress is cleared, it becomes easier to come back into balance and cultivate a healthy second response.

Questions To Facilitate Your Inner Exploration

1. Remember a time when you reacted from your first response. Remember how you felt emotionally. Remember how you felt physically in your body. How did the reaction effect the situation? Can you remember feeling that way before? In childhood? In adult life?

2. Reflect to determine what could have been a healthier second response.

3. Think of some additional examples from your life.

First and Second Responses in Your Personal Relationships

There are many New Age, self-help, and psychotherapeutic circles that call the relationship between you and your spouse the crucible where all of your issues are going to come up. Furthermore, by intensely working on that with your spouse and digging into your first responses, you're going to become self-improved. The reality is that what you're going to become is divorced.

I went to see a spiritual teacher from India, and somebody asked him about relationships. I liked his response. He said, "I only have three things to say about relationships. Number one, relationships should be easy. Number two, relationships should be easy. And number three, relationships should be easy." The way you're going to make relationships easy is by cultivating a healthy second response. It's not by speaking "your truth" in that moment of rage.

There is such a thing as an "unhealthy" second response. A common example has occurred in many American households over the past fifty years, but fortunately is declining. A rough, aggressive, and controlling husband comes home and bosses his wife around until he goes to the bed. The wife feels angry, used, and abused, but she has an unhealthy second response that says, "Well, I'm going to keep peace in the home. I'm just going to keep my mouth shut since speaking up doesn't work anyway." That's an unhealthy second response.

A healthy second response has nothing to do with denial or suppressing the feeling the situation provokes. It has to do with coming into balance. It comes from exploring the nature of the feeling, where it came from, what it's about, if it is based in projection or perception, whether or not it would be life-supporting to bring it up, and how to bring it up in a life supporting and constructive manner. When you're in balance, and you've cultivated a healthy second response, you bring it to your spouse and say, "Let's talk about this." How you do so requires a level of wisdom. You have to find an appropriate time and way to say it. But you don't just stuff it. Stuffing it is not a healthy second response.

I've seen many relationships destroyed by self-help groups founded in the notion that "speaking your truth," means blaring out your first response.

So it's crucial to explore our relationship with, not just what we hear on television, but also with what we learn from self help workshops and books. Some workshops and books can serve by showing you examples of what you wouldn't want to do. In that sense, they act as catalysts to strengthening your own inner knowing. You can learn from them in that way.

Chapter 2

Day Two:
Doorways to Your Psyche

In Day One you were introduced to the fundamentals. In Day Two, you'll enter the terrain of your inner landscape. You'll do this by exploring some examples of what I call an "in." "Ins" are like doorways through which you go to access and bring healing to your inner psyche. I mentioned a few in Day One, such as exploring your childhood conditioning and exploring your first and second response. Today you'll explore some very powerful "ins:" your transference and what I call *The Five Divine Currents*™.

Transference

Transference is how the mind functions. The mind is conditioned, or programmed, as a result of the psychophysiological impact of previous life experiences. The experiences, especially those from childhood, create impressions that we project on to the world. That projection is called transference. The projection of your subconscious beliefs about men is an example of transference. These beliefs are largely influenced by your experiences with your father. They may be positive or negative beliefs. When you go out into the world and look at men, you may subconsciously say to yourself, "I know what men are like because I knew my dad. He was a man and all men are like that." Similarly, your experiences with your mother create impressions on your psyche that lead to your subconscious beliefs about women. As a result, whenever you interact with a woman you unconsciously project those impressions onto her.

We have impressions concerning everything: authority figures, work, play, marriage, life in general, and so on. When we walk into a room, we don't just perceive the room, we perceive on to the room. Our experience of the room is a function of our transference stemming from our past impressions.

Many psychotherapists believe, "I'm a psychotherapist. I've done a lot of work with my transference, so I'm not in transference anymore." That is simply not true. What has happened is the psychotherapists are now transferring new identities about people, the psyche, and even transference itself, on to their clients and the rest of the world. They're still in transference. They still perceive on to whatever it is they perceive. In fact, everybody is in transference. We're all always in transference. So mental health is not a matter of getting rid of transference. What is it about?

It's about cultivating a healthy relationship with your transference. When you rest in the place inside of you that dwells beyond the grasp of transference, you no longer lose yourself to your transference. Instead you give your transference more space. You don't know for certain if your experience is your transference or clear perception, but it really doesn't matter because you're not white-knuckled either way. You don't identify with being free of transference. You have a healthy relationship with how you experience things. You're open to working with that relationship without being rigidly fixed or numb to your experiences.

You cultivate a healthy relationship with your transference by exploring your inner landscape. In fact, exploring your transference is a great way to facilitate your inner exploration because it is so fundamental to how your psyche works. You and I are in transference right now. You can do your inner exploration at any moment by asking yourself, "How am I in transference right now?" Your life is a transferential dance around the purity that lies at the depth of your being. The underlying motivation is pure and divine, but your transferential dance around that ranges from your deeper truths to your most superficial first responses.

Question: How do we deal with our first responses? My parents are both scientists. When I was a child, they always forced their logic on me. It drove me nuts! I would just go into confusion. That was my first response. I couldn't help it.

We deal with our first responses by having a healthy relationship with them. We don't act on them blindly, but give them space. We have a healthy relationship with our whole process. We have a healthy relationship with any sort of intellectual paradigm. That is, we also don't lose ourselves when our various paradigms contradict. At the same time, we don't white knuckle on to one paradigm or the other. We give space to the contradictions. Paradox and contradiction is inherent to the nature of the universe. For example, the aphorisms, "Everything is well and wisely put; it's all God's will," and "You have to get out there and make things happen; nothing worthwhile happens on its own," can be experienced as a perplexing contradiction. White knuckling to either perspective gets you into trouble.

Just be easy with the process. Give it space and feel your way. Then you'll know what to do. You'll know which perspective to align with. It'll just feel like common sense. When you really start feeling that place within your being, somebody can come to you, force his logic upon you, and say, "This is the way it is," and you won't get buried. You won't lose yourself to the perspective they are trying to impose upon your awareness.

However, if you habitually impose perspectives upon your awareness and don't give your head any space, you're going to be very susceptible when somebody else does that to you. You got that habit from your parents. That's what they did to you, so now that's what you do to yourself. The way you treat yourself is the way you experience everyone else treating you. As you explore this issue, you will develop a different relationship with your intellect and logic. You'll realize that logic is a great tool, but a poor master.

For example, suppose your friend tells you that it's natural to walk around naked. After all, a human body is simply a human body. Furthermore, your friend argues that the people who aren't willing to walk down the street naked simply have hang-ups about their bodies. After really hearing what your friend has to say, you can sit back and think, "The logic may be sound, but so what?" You haven't lost yourself to the logic and decided to take off your clothes and walk down the street.

Instead you feel there is another reality—reality that you feel inside your being. Based on that feeling you begin to create specific words to give voice to your inner experience. Words like "dignity" and "cultural integrity" may appear as your response to public nudity. When your deeper truths, what I call "fine feelings," start communicating with your intellect, the right person is in the driver's seat. You are now feeling your way instead of thinking

your way. You act from your deeper second response arising from a deeper truth, instead of some intellectual justi-
fication arising from a conditioned response. As you
develop more inner space through the exploration of your
psychodynamic landscape, you naturally begin to deal
with your first response in a responsible way.

Transference makes the world go around.
Transference isn't something that beginners do and
advanced people don't do. Everybody does it.
Transference is the medium through which we do the
dance called life. When you walk into a room, you always
perceive on to the room. It's the way our psychophysiology works. It's the way we interface with existence.

But the question is how intense is its grip? Some say
you become an observer of your transference, but others
say if you're observing it, it is no longer transference. In
fact, we could define transference to be the basis of the
conditioned workings of our psyche that we are oblivious
to. But the oblivion dominates our being to varying
degrees. As we become more and more mentally healthy,
the fullness of our own being dominates over the oblivion.
We are like a kite. With a strong sense of inner being acting as a tail, we no longer spin out of control at the mercy
of our transference.

Question: So in a sense we move beyond our transference?

Transference is always there, but if you don't have a
solid base in self, you spin like a kite without a tail.

As we purify our physiology, the stress in our physiology diminishes and we loosen our white-knuckled attachment to our transference. Transference still happens—it's the dance we do. We just lose ourselves to it less and less. We know it for what it is, neither good nor bad, but just the nature of our personality. When you're grounded in the depth of your own being, you ride the wind of transference, but you're not compromised by it. It's as if your impressions are a superficial veil, lightly etched on the surface of your being. You still spontaneously do your dance, but you're grounded in your own fullness. This fullness is the source of common sense, wisdom, happiness, and productivity in life. Instead of living your life based on your transference, you live it *through* your transference but based upon your fullness.

Question: So inside there is a sense that everything is perfect?

You could say that, but you're not overtaken by the notion that everything is perfect. In other words, even as you become more grounded in your self and flow more smoothly with your deeper nature, you still have affinities and aversions stemming from your personality. Although these affinities and aversions are an intimate part of your nature, they do not enslave you.

Question: So it's like you are in the world, but not of it?

You can say it that way. But what does that even mean? The problem is that wise people have said this sort of thing throughout the ages. Religions have been born around such statements, but nobody really understands them. The understanding is subtle. If you look at those teachings with sincere intent and a discerning eye, you start to realize that maybe you don't really understand what the spiritual teachings actually mean. A big component of effective personal process is humility. As soon as we conclude that we are masters of our transference, we are identified with that concept and we transfer that onto everything and everyone else. It's just that subtle. It's just that sublime. We even give that space. We have an idea of what "identified with" and "not identified with" means, but only obscurely. We explore it more and develop more feeling for it, but we never grab on to it and conclude, "Here is where I'm identified, and there is where I am not." Life is elusive by nature. It's subtle. It's sublime.

Question: I'm feeling a little frustrated. This is getting confusing.

The more you look at it the subtler it gets. I guess I prefer the word "subtle" to "confusing." It keeps getting more and more subtle. Your relationship with that subtlety is crucial. If you give space to your inner landscape, your relationship with it feels good and facilitates your inner exploration. If you get upset and say to yourself, "I don't really understand what this guy is saying," you undermine your relationship with the subtle nature of life itself. If you try to hang on to a definition of your inner workings that's too clear, you compromise the exploration. That is the nature of existence and the nature of your inner landscape. You need to give space to your inner landscape. Otherwise, you try to grab on to who you are and then suddenly, as a result, that's not who you are anymore. It's just some notion, an identity. That's the way life works. I'm not trying to be metaphysical here. I'm just discussing the way it works. It's the nature of the human psyche.

Question: So are philosophy, physics, and religion all components of psychology?

Consider the statement, "You can't take heaven by storm." It's a universal principle. You can apply it in many ways, including to what we just said. You can't grab onto your inner landscape—it slips through your fingers. It's a subtle fabric. If you try to freeze it, it becomes an identity. Life is that way, and so is the fine fabric of your inner being. Biblical verses relate to the way the human psyche is structured. When interpreted in that context, they make beautiful sense.

Question: What about the idea of karma?

You could say that your karma is the stress in your physiology, if you like.

Questions To Facilitate Your Inner Exploration

1. Can you think of someone who in some way reminds you of your mother? Who? Explain.

2. Now, how about your father?

3. Can you feel how you may have projected (trans-

ferred) qualities of your mother or father onto this person? If so, what qualities? Describe these qualities.

4. What qualities do you tend to project onto men? Onto women? Onto minority groups? Onto authority figures? Onto the rich or poor? etc.

The Five Divine Currents

Psychologists have identified innumerable models of the human psyche. Remember they are only of practical value to the extent that they facilitate your own inner exploration. You abuse them if you employ them to label yourself or others. One model that I feel has great practical value, I call *The Five Divine Currents*™.

Certain attributes, or currents, lie at the depth of every individual's being, attributes of their purity. These currents are spirituality (affinity for the ethereal), love, sensitivity, commitment, and impeccability. They are all very positive attributes. For example, it is good to be sensitive (sensitivity current) to your own inner feelings as well as to other people. Also, the desire to do things properly (the impeccability current) is a laudable quality. These five different attributes are inherent to the depth of everyone's deepest inner nature.

I like to compare them to incense sticks. When incense first starts to burn in a still room, the smoke goes up straight and pure. As the smoke begins to experience slight drafts in the air, it begins to twist and swirl. Like that, the laudable attributes of our inner being begin to twist and swirl as we experience worldly life and incur stress in our psychophysiology. The stresses manifest as conditionings and identities in the psyche. Some of the currents may go up relatively straight, and some of them may get severely convoluted. But it's important to realize that whatever dance we do, our essential nature is pure. It's all a dance around these very positive attributes.

Remember, individuals tend to have more conditionings and identities around some of these currents than around others. People sometimes have conditioning predominately around a combination of two. But we all have some conditioning around all five.

Sigmund Freud developed the cognitive approach to psychotherapy: an analytical and intellectual approach. In this approach, the therapist heals the client by figuring out what makes him tick. A psychologist named Wilhelm Reich, a colleague of Freud's, disagreed with Freud. According to Reich, to heal a wound, it must be felt in the body. It's not enough to think about the psychodynamic landscape. One must also feel it in his body. From Reich's work, his student Alexander Lowen, founder of Bioenergetic Analysis, developed an understanding of five developmentally-based character types.

The flaw in the approach of Reich and Lowen is that it is out/in. Because it defines people based on the outer manifestations of their behavioral patterns, it is a convoluted understanding. The therapist that uses this approach loses sight of the client's deeper nature, the basis of who the client is. The therapist loses touch with the fact that there's only one inner motivation at work: to commune, that is, to love. Anything in life that doesn't appear to be love is just love in a confused state. To really understand the client, the therapist needs to see him in that context. If the therapist looks at the client in terms of a character type, a wounded being that is oral, psychopathic, rigid, masochistic, or schizoid, the therapist is missing the essential point. That's why I came up with *The Five Divine Currents.*

As you read about *The Five Divine Currents*, remember that love is the basis of all action and the underlying force of the human psyche. In that sense, we could say that universal love underlies all five currents. It's the fountainhead and we could view the currents as branching off from it. When it comes right down to it, there's only one thing that everyone in this room wants and that's love. By love I mean communion, unification, and merging, not just with other people, but with everything. Not in an emotional sense or an immature sense, but in a very refined and ultimate sense; in the deepest sense of the word "communion." That's what everyone wants.

We present the currents in a particular order (first spirituality, then love, sensitivity, commitment, and finally, impeccability) because they tend to appear in that order as an individual develops. Conditioning around the spirituality current tends to manifest the earliest, around the time of

birth. The love current conditioning tends to manifest a little later, during the time the baby is breastfeeding.
Conditioning around the sensitivity current tends to manifest when the individual is around two years old.
Conditioning around the commitment current tends to
manifest around age three or four, and conditioning around
the impeccability current tends to manifest around age five.

The Spirituality Current

To feel your spirituality current does not require you
to be religious or to even believe in God, although that is
how most people feel their spirituality. Spirituality dwells
in all of us as a sense of our universality. We feel our love
for and communion with the exquisiteness of universal life
and nature including the sky above, the earth below, and
the community of all living and nonliving things. People
can feel it when they extend their arms over their heads and
reach for the heavens above, when they hear an exquisite
symphony, when they go to church, or when they look out
at a sunset over the ocean. It brings us to an expanded
sense of our own being, which lies far beyond worldly
affairs and physical concerns. It is associated with a lofty,
pristine, eternal sense of our own consciousness, as individuals as well as the family of humanity. To feel it has
inspired a sense of personified universal love many call
God. It includes the feeling of being looked over and cared
for by God, having a personal relationship with divinity.

Conditioning around the spirituality current tends to

occur *in utero* or around the time of birth. Many traumas can lead to that conditioning. For example, the mother might feel stressed during pregnancy so the child also feels stressed. Maybe conditions in the womb were not ideal, instilling within the child the fear to exist or be alive. To this child, the very feeling of being embodied is associated with the emotion of fear. The birthing process may have been very difficult so the infant does not want to be in that body. It's experienced as an unpleasant place to be.

So where do they go? In a sense they try to get out of their body. As adults, they tend to be floating away as if into an ethereal spirit world. People with a great deal of stress around the spirituality current look like their aware-ness is up at the top of the ceiling. I remember a high school friend who walked around like that all the time. We had a joke: I'd walk by him in the hallway and say "Hi, Irvin," and wave to the ceiling above his head. He'd reply, "Hi, Michael," and wave up to the ceiling also. Because they are not fully connected to the body, the body tends to be thin and lacking "charge," although it doesn't have to be—other currents could be lively too. Often there are left/right imbalances, as if they're trying to spiral and squirm out of the body. They have a far away look in their eye. If you touch their feet, they tend to feel cold, hollow, and empty as if nobody's at home.

People with stress around the spirituality current tend to be highly mental; they don't want to feel things in their bodies. They don't want to go out in the world. They're identified with an internal world of mental or spiritual notions, so they can have an attitude of superiority: "I'm beyond mundane and earthly stuff."

The spirituality current trauma is associated with fear. To be alive in the physical world is terrifying. For someone with stress around the spirituality current, it could be terrifying to go up to the ticket counter and buy a ticket for a movie. There is too much connection with somebody they don't know.

Psychophysiological conditioning carries with it a double bind. Those with stress around the spirituality current are confronted with the double bind, "If I exist I die. To exist in a body is to die." There's no way out.

Question: I guess this is sort of a silly question, but I'm feeling sort of depressed. Why does life have to be filled with such difficulties as these?

Once you go through the whole exploration, life feels like such a treasure! What you find out is that you're fine. You're exquisite. What a relief! It would be a really lousy world if some of us were truly jerks! That won't happen. I promise. It's built into the very mechanics of life. There's no such thing as a Darth Vader in any ultimate sense. When Darth Vader works out all his conditionings and identities, he'll find out that he's divine. Interestingly enough, that is actually how it turned out at the end of the Star Wars trilogy.

The Love Current

Universal love is at the basis of all the currents. By "love current" we specifically mean the love for another embodied being or beings. It is usually thought of as love for another person, but also includes love for a pet. It is interpersonal love. It is that fine, tender, precious feeling we feel for another. It gives meaning to our worldly life and fills our hearts with overflowing fullness in communion and appreciation for the recipient of our love. It has been and will always be the source of inspiration for countless songs, poems, and stories. This includes the songs, poems, and stories of our daily lives as we live with one and other in the communion of interpersonal love.

Conditioning around the love current usually occurs while the infant is breastfeeding, right after conditioning around the spirituality current occurs. The work of the British analyst, D. W. Winnecott, provides some good insights on how this conditioning occurs. Winnecott spent a lot of time observing babies with their mothers and realized that in the beginning there is no such thing as baby and mother. The child doesn't feel separate from the mother; it just feels the oneness of baby/mother. As the mother holds and feeds the child during those early months of breastfeeding, the child starts to develop a sense of a holding space. In this holding space, the infant feels safe and can rest into its own body, its own being.

Winnecott also originated the concept of the "good enough mother." According to Winnecott, the best mother is not a perfect mother who holds her child perfectly all the time. It's good for the development of the child that the mother has to go away, even if it's only to go to the bathroom, because during the brief moments she is gone, the child learns how to hold itself in that holding space. If the mother is away too long, the child begins to feel unsafe. If the mother holds the child perfectly at all times, the child does not have the opportunity to learn how to hold itself, to rest into its own being independently from the mother. Winnecott observed that this "individuation process" continues as the child grows older. The child begins to discover its autonomy from its mother and a separate identity.

Transitional objects such as a baby blanket or a teddy bear can ease the process. These objects act as a substitute for the mother so the child can learn to rest in its being when she is not around. As adults, we still have our transitional objects, such as Archie Bunker's chair or a favorite piece of jewelry.

The child continues the transition as it gets older and begins to enjoy greater autonomy. You have probably seen a toddler run across the room, turn to make sure Mommy is still there, and then run off again. The child is weaning himself from his mother, and learning to rest in his own being.

A group of psychotherapists tried to heal their clients using a technique based upon Winnecott's teachings. They reasoned that their clients' lives were a mess because they did not have a strong sense of their inner holding space. The Winnecott devotees decided to recreate a holding space for their clients. So they provided constancy. They never changed the furniture arrangement. If they put a cup by the client's chair during the client's first visit, it would be there every time. Every session, the client would sit in the same chair next to the same cup. If the therapist planned a vacation, she'd tell her client two years in advance and remind the client at every session. This way, the client could really count on the reliability of the therapist.

The clients got better. Their lives started coming together as long as the constancy of their therapists holding space was there. However, when the therapist retired or died, her clients fell apart. The therapists found that their holding space was no substitute for the holding space the child gets from the "good enough mother." The approach was abandoned because the clients did not learn how to rest into themselves when the therapist wasn't around. They only became dependent on the therapist.

If an infant is not emotionally fed during its breastfeeding stage, stress develops around the love current. The stress influences the physical characteristics the person carries into adult life. Because the body isn't getting emotionally nourished it tends to be small. The chest tends to be caved in because the heart wasn't filled. The jaw might also be pulled in and small because the person's emotions were insufficiently fed. Remember that these are just tendencies, not absolute rules.

As adults, people with conditioning around the love current feel empty and wanting. Their eyes tend to have a wanting and sucking look. When you are around them, they seem to pull at you or suck on you. In their relationships, they look for someone to fill the void inside, to no avail. Their unspoken statement is "You must give it to me. You owe it to me. You're not taking care of me. But if you do give it to me, you won't do it right anyway." But they may shroud that with another unspoken statement: "I don't need, I won't ask." They feel that, "If I have to ask for your love, it's not really love," and at the same time, "If I don't ask for your love, I won't get it." It's a painful double bind.

People with conditioning around the love current haven't fully discovered their own inner fullness. Through exploration, they realize that, within their own being, they are full.

There is a part of each of us that can resonate with conditioning around all five currents. Finding that part inside of you and exploring it is a powerful tool for your personal process.

It is important to keep in mind that experiences from childhood are exactly that: what it was like to the child, not what actually happened. Conditioning around the love current doesn't necessarily mean the mother was negligent. From the perspective of an outside witness, her behavior may or may not have coincided with the child's experience.

The Sensitivity Current

The exquisiteness of our sensitivity current includes our ability to feel the presence and feelings of another person deeply within our own being. It involves compassion for others, as well as an acute body felt sense awareness to the presence and influence of another. It includes the intuitive and visceral ability to deeply feel someone's state of heart and mind and the impact that state has on our self and others. This sense inspires kindness and tenderness toward others. It includes the instinct to reach out and touch another to offer comfort and support.

The primary period of conditioning around the sensitivity current occurs when the child is exploring their autonomy from mother, around the time of the "terrible twos." Conditioning around the sensitivity current occurs when the mother is experienced as invasive. Maybe the mother says, "Eat your food, here have another piece of bread, eat more food, eat." The feeling of invasion is at both ends. "Let's change your diaper. Here's an enema. You didn't go to the bathroom. Let's take your temperature (with a rectal thermometer)." The mother might be domineering.

Children who experience this tend to become hypersensitive and pinch off their throat and buttocks, including the space between their thighs. They also tend to pull their throat, neck, and shoulders up and close together. They accumulate body mass to protect themselves from being invaded, but it doesn't work. In fact, people look at their size, think there is no way to get through to them, and try harder, which only leads to more invasion. Those with sensitivity current conditioning act with the underlying motivation: "If I can take it, if I let Mommy feed me and change my diaper and I don't complain or cause her any trouble, then I'm good." So they grow up being good and able to take just about anything. If you load the wagon they'll pull it. You don't even have to load it; they'll load it for you.

People with sensitivity current conditioning walk around feeling very sensitive to the world. Others look at them and think, "They're so big, you couldn't hurt them with a Mack truck," but the very opposite is true. They are sensitive to almost everything. They have a great deal of love, very "big hearts," and feel that the way to show that love is by being accommodating. They become identified with being accommodating and taking on whatever anybody gives them, however invasive it may feel, and lose touch with their own wanting. They want whatever Mommy wants them to want.

Question: Is the conditioning around these currents always related to the mother?

No. It's generally related to the primary caretaker, who is usually the mother. When we get to the commitment and impeccability currents, fathers begin to have more influence.

In response to the continual experience of invasion, those with conditioning around the sensitivity current have a great deal of pent up rage. They are furious that they have been invaded. A pressure builds up from the suppression of their natural flow. When the pressure is released, it comes out as rage. Then they are humiliated by their display of rage. If they show the rage, they are humiliated, but if they don't show it they are humiliated by the constant invasion. Either way they are humiliated. That is the double bind around the sensitivity current.

The Commitment Current

Love that inspires dedication to a cause gives rise to the commitment current. The cause can vary from individual to universal. It can be in service of God, country, truth, justice, ethics, family, self or another. It includes the qualities of righteousness, honor, devoutness, allegiance, and piety.

Around age four, conditioning around the commitment current can start to take place. Sometimes these later currents are discussed in terms of sex. In my opinion, this is correct in some cases, but not all. Conditioning around the commitment current takes place when the kid is coerced into playing the role of an adult before he or she is ready. He has to be a little man before he's ready or she has to be a little woman before she's ready. Some ways a child can be coerced into playing an adult's role include being made to take care of the younger siblings because the parents are unavailable or needing to protect the younger sibling from an abusive parent.

From a sexual perspective, sometimes the mother and father didn't get along so the mother makes the little boy her "little man." Daddy turns the little girl into his substitute female companion. A mother might even complain to her son about her rotten husband and say, "I'm glad you're not like your Daddy, Joey." Consequently, little Joey starts to puff up and try to be Mommy's little man before he's ready.

Daddy's little girl learns to present her little cute face, arrange her hair the way her father likes, wear her nice little blouses, and be just right as Daddy's little woman.

Men with commitment current conditioning often have big upper bodies because they're puffing up and trying to be big. However, something subtle about their walk might look like that of a little boy because they tried to "walk like a man" before they were ready. You have probably seen some of them walking shirtless up and down the beach; they have big upper bodies, little disconnected legs, and tiny little butts.

Because they had to take charge as an adult before they were ready, people with conditioning around the commitment current must be right and do things right. So their war cry becomes "I'm right, you're wrong." Yet inside they feel they were betrayed by their mothers and fathers, the very people they loved the most. As a result, they are angry and vow to never be betrayed again. They never allow betrayal to happen to anyone anywhere. As adults, they try to right wrongs. Their life becomes a series of fights for causes, especially their own.

While conditioning around the commitment current takes place, the child experiences tremendous power. For example, "Mommy's little man" and "Daddy's little girl" learn to manipulate their parents. As they get older they tend to be very manipulative. They can display their manipulative ability in different ways. They can be confrontational. They can be underground, manipulating things in a subtle way. They can be seductive. They may be pleasing you and doing everything you want them to do, but they're playing you like a violin and you don't even know it. They're getting their way across the board. That's the dance around the commitment current.

The Impeccability Current

We love. Inherent to the consummate purity of that love is the desire to behave, give, and do in faultless service of that perfect love. We strive to live our lives as an ideal expression of the flawless purity of that love. That is the beautiful expression of the impeccability current.

The following illustrates the classical perspective of the impeccability current: Daddy loves his little girl and everything's fine. But one day she jumps up on his lap and hugs him. It feels good and there's a lot of love until suddenly Daddy starts to notice that she's actually a sexual being. This makes him feel uncomfortable. The next time the little girl jumps up on his lap, he pushes her off because he can't deal with the possibility that he's sexually attracted to his little girl. As a result, she feels rejected and gets the message, "It is not okay to have feelings," or "As soon as you start looking like a woman you can't have love." This can also happen between mother and son.

When the girl grows up she can have sex, but not sex and love at the same time. The experience of love and sex are disconnected. She grows ashamed of her love, and can't show it because she'll get rejected. She learns to hold her love inside, hidden and still, while she maintains an organized and rigid appearance. Her longing for love becomes a very tender, delicate, and frail flower that she won't show.

In reality, conditioning around the impeccability current can be created in other ways. For example, very disciplinary military parents might tell their four year old, "You've got to step in line and do it perfectly." This shuts down the child's love. I've seen a lot of people with conditioning around the impeccability current come from families where the father is in the military and disciplines them from day one. The child's natural and spontaneous expression of love is rejected.

People identified with the impeccability current have to be perfect. They tend to hold themselves perfectly. It's not uncommon when you first meet such people to think they are perfect. They appear perfect because nothing else is acceptable. Nothing else is safe. The irony here is that they're very sensitive, but others are often rude to them and resent them for being so perfect. It feels like an ice pick going right through their delicate hearts. Thus, the pain of their childhood is recreated. But of course, they can't show it.

Be careful when you apply the *The Five Divine Currents* model. People tend to use it to define themselves. For example, they conclude, "Oh, I'm wounded around the sensitivity current." But know that this is just a stage in the understanding of the model that many go through. This model is a tool for your exploration that is ab-used if you define yourself or other people with it. Everybody has conditioning around all five of the currents. The conditioning does not define who you are. As you cultivate a refined relationship with this model, you will find it's true purpose is to facilitate the exploration of your inner landscape.

During this early stage, avoid the temptation to say to your spouse, "Oh you are a commitment current. Now I know who you are. Now I know exactly why you are the way you are." We want to get past this stage as quickly as we can. The purpose of our work here isn't to judge ourselves and others, put everyone in boxes, and congratulate ourselves for our deep insights. The purpose of our work here is to help us under-stand, not over-stand. So if you find yourself standing over your spouse using *The Five Divine Currents* model, you're missing the point. You would do well to under-stand more.

Questions To Facilitate Your Inner Exploration

1. Reflect on your life in terms of *The Five Divine Currents*.

2. Think of people who you know that illustrate conditioning around each of the currents. Remember this is only a learning exercise. Do not misuse this knowledge by labeling people.

Chapter 3

Day Three:
Strengthening Your Inner Being

Understanding psychological health is one thing. Achieving it is another. In Day Three you will apply what you have learned so far. As we discuss various subjects, explore your "relationship with" not only me and how you feel about what I am saying, but more importantly your "relationship with" what is going on inside of you. This process will strengthen your inner sense of self.

Sex and Sexuality

Human Sexuality, the classic text by Masters and Johnson, says that every human being experiences periods of heterosexuality, asexuality, and homosexuality. I think that statement alone gives people some space around their sexual urges and periods of sexual aversion or affinity.

Our culture provides little space in the arena of sexuality, as illustrated by the typical late night talk show that depicts sexual health as having sex ten times a week. As a result, many people feel a great deal of pressure around their sexuality. For example, if someone does not feel sexually inclined for a period of time, he and his partner are likely to judge him harshly.

The teen years are a particularly confusing time from a sexual point of view. The physiology is changing. The hormones are surging. Peer pressures are powerful. Based upon a single sexual experience, teens often label themselves a prude, tramp, gay, asexual, and so on. Teens often give themselves no space whatsoever. They jump to a conclusion, start acting on it, and paint themselves into a corner. As a result, I've seen teens get terribly confused.

When someone decides (perhaps from parental pressure) to be a priest or some kind of spiritual celibate, another form of giving no space around sexuality can occur. He thinks, "I'm going to be the highest, most honorable thing I can be. I'm going to be a priest." He claims a celibate lifestyle that is not his nature and gives himself no space as a result. The church gives him no space either, and he spends years trying to align with that lifestyle. So sooner or later, this healthy heterosexual living an asexual lifestyle ends up snapping and abusing some kid in the church. This essentially very good person ends up doing a horrible thing because he did not give himself the space necessary to rest into his true nature.

Question: Do you see many people who you feel are sexually healthy?

In the arena of sexuality, there are few people who give themselves space. I am not advocating a sexually free experimental lifestyle because when people do that they end up painting themselves into another corner. The space I'm talking about is not an external one where you try this and try that to find out what you like and what you do not. Instead, it is an internal space where you can just rest into who you sexually are.

Society makes giving space a challenging task. It may be politically correct to *say* there is nothing wrong if you are homosexual, but there is often little space given to the psyche regarding homosexuality. And if someone is going through a period of asexuality, it seems to be politically correct to assume that there is something unhealthy about the person. That is just not true.

As we explore our psyche in every arena, including sexuality, we naturally begin to give ourselves more internal space to be who we are. So the way to give yourself space around anything is to explore your relationship with it.

Trying to Turn Apples Into Oranges

In psychotherapy, what is done in the name of self-improvement often amounts to what I call "turning apples into oranges." For example, suppose the tree in our backyard is looking rather sickly. Its roots have curved around a formation of rocks as it grew. We want to save this tree, so we fertilize it and make sure it gets enough water. As a result, the tree becomes stronger and begins to flourish. But it is still curved. However, the curves are a beautiful aspect of its nature. Our personalities are like the tree. We each curve in our own ways: exquisite expressions of our unique personalities. Can you imagine a forest of trees all growing out of the ground as perfect two-by-fours? The thought is ridiculous. Yet many people strive to form their personalities into perfect two-by-fours and call it self-improvement!

Our personal process is not about trying to become psychological Barbie and Ken dolls. Personal process is about tilling the soil, so that we can rest into the exquisite curves and contours unique to our own nature. Our inner nature is always something delightfully wonderful. As we explore it, we spontaneously begin to act in a more life-supporting manner. The curves do not need to come out. If you feel the need to change your personality, so be it. But do it with the knowledge that it is not the healing.

Questions To Facilitate Your Inner Exploration

1. Can you think of someone who has manipulated their personality to such an extent that they feel to you like they are playing a role of some kind?

2. Can you think of someone who has done so many years of personal process work that they just don't seem real any longer, like they are playing a role? Please describe.

3. In what ways may you have manipulated your personality so that you will behave a particular way?

4. Consider the possibility that you have somehow compromised your true nature in doing so.

Your Center

Your center is the place where your being is focused. To illustrate the concept, I like to tell a story about my friend I'll refer to as Sharon. When she looked at a door, you felt that her entire being was over at the door. When I talked to her, it felt like she was right in my face, even if she was standing ten feet away. Wherever Sharon's attention went, that's where her center went. Her center was right in the middle of her object of perception.

I once held up my hand and as she looked at my palm, her center went right to it. I explained that to her and asked her if she could feel it. She wasn't sure but she thought she could. Then, as I slowly moved my hand toward Sharon's face I asked her if she could feel her center moving closer to her face. She said that she could. As I continued to move my hand closer to her face she was able to feel her center move more and more clearly. Then I invited Sharon to bring that feeling iside of her chest and into her heart. You should have seen her light up with joy from the experience.

I then directed her to move her center into her upper and then lower abdomen. I suggested that she take a moment or two each day to notice where her center was. As time passed, Sharon became very thankful. She felt that her relationship with her center had become much healthier and said that she finally felt comfortable in her body.

There are different schools of thought that describe where the center has to be. The Buddhist talk about the heart cave, and about remaining centered in the heart. The Chinese martial artists hold the notion that the center, the *dan tien*, is supposed to be in the lower abdomen. One self-help guru calls the center the "core star" and says it is 3 inches below the heart. Other people insist the center is a couple inches above the belly button. There are many conflicting opinions about where you should keep your center. I have noticed that it is very strange to be around someone who tries to keep his or her center fixed in one place. It feels very unnatural.

Yet the notion of center is a good one. It can really facilitate your inner exploration just to notice where you tend to be centered. Where are you centered right now? Where do you tend to be centered while at work? Where do you tend to be centered when you are resting at home?

The point I would like to make about the center is that it is suppose to move. It is natural for it to move. This whole idea about trying to stay centered in your heart cave, your *dan tien*, or your core star is all wrong. When you're cuddled up in a blanket on a cold winter night with a nice bowl of chicken soup, you're probably centered right in your tummy and feeling all warm and fuzzy. If a door slams with a bang, it's normal, for a moment, for your center to shift to the door. Talking to a little child, you may find yourself centered right in you heart. The center is supposed to move.

It can be a valuable thing from time to time to notice the place where you're centered. Maybe you'll notice, "Oh my goodness, I'm across the room," or "I'm always in my head." Maybe you will feel inclined to move your center around for a moment and see what feels most comfortable and natural. That exploration can facilitate the self-correcting mechanism. That's healing. Trying to hold it anywhere is identifying with an overlay.

The Three Essentials of Healing

The first essential of the healing process is the self-correcting mechanism. Due to its inherent nature, the seed grows into a tree. You do not have to tell it how to grow. Likewise, inherent in your being is the inner intelligence that directs your psychodynamic healing, if you allow it to.

The second essential of healing is exploration, the tilling of the soil. Simply loosening the soil around the roots facilitates a plant's development. As you explore your inner psychodynamic structure with all the tools described in this book (your life story, your history as a child, motivation, center, inner space, self-honesty, and so on), you till the soil of your inner self, which enables the self-correcting mechanism to do its work.

The third essential of healing is commonly called "the holding space," but "resting space" is a better term. This is a sense of resting into your inner being. The reason we do our personal process is to awaken this resting space. It is that place you rest into in the depth of your own self that gives context and foundation to your life. It is like the anchor of a ship or the tail of a kite. It is the source of inner order at the basis of the self-correcting mechanism.

The whole purpose of psychotherapy is to rest more fully into the holding space at the depth of your being. When you rest into and live from the depth of your being, you're mentally healthy. A healthy relationship with all the different paradigms, all the different possibilities in life, is based upon that place of inner wisdom you rest in. Self-awareness, self-esteem, and self-worth come from resting into that inner space. It is the source of your inner strength. Everyone has at least some sense of that place. Without any sense of it, we have no mental or physical health at all.

The inner strength you derive from the holding space is essential to your personal process and healing. To do your inner exploration requires some inner strength and courage. People are often afraid to look within. Not knowing what they might find can be terrifying.

You can support the holding space by giving yourself inner space around your inner mental processes. It also helps to know that you are not limited to your personality. You may not want to look at the inner landscape of your personality because you think your personality is who you are. That is not who you are. It's just what you've been up to lately. Your personality is not the essence of your being. Who you are lies much deeper than the personality level.

Question: Can a therapist create a holding space for his or her client?

Yes, in a sense, a therapist can. A therapist can help to create a holding space by creating a safe and comfortable environment for the client. But this is an exterior holding space. The vital holding space is the client's inner resting space. The client cultivates this space as he becomes more mentally healthy. The holding space a therapist creates is superficial, and acts as a temporary support.

Question: How can we do it for ourselves?

That starts with a healthy relationship with your psychodynamic process: your current issues are not about who you are, or what is wrong with you. They are just what you've been holding on to.

Question: Can meditation help?

Proper meditation can directly enliven the resting space. Exploration helps us till the soil of our inner being. Through the exploration, we can take a look at how we've been white knuckling to our identities—our affinities and aversions—even the ones we hold thinking that they keep us healthy and safe. Holding, in that sense, is what blocks our psychodynamic health.

Question: Once I see what is wrong or unhealthy about the way my psyche works, what do I do about it?

Personal process is about getting out of the way of the self-correcting mechanism. What gets in the way is holding on to notions, ideas, attitudes, and perspectives. Some of our holdings are intellectual, and some are emotional. They can run very deep in our being. They become the things that make us feel secure, give us an identity, tell us who we are, and give us a sense of self, albeit a false one. Who you are is like the idle of a car. It's that deep full restful space that dwells at the depth of your psyche. It's that quality of the nervous system when it's purring, when it's free of stress, when it's no longer holding on to identities. Some people call it their soul.

Question: Do we hold in other places of our being other than the nervous system as a result of stress?

Yes. We hold on all levels of our being. We hold in our muscles, in our organs, in every cell, and in our psyches. Each part of our being affects the other. Releasing the holding in the muscles or the tissues has a positive effect on the psyche.

Self-honesty

To really get in touch with what is going on within your psyche requires self-honesty. Are you holding on so tightly to your identities and your sense of self-esteem that you don't want to admit it? Are you so afraid or ashamed of your self-perceived flaws that you avoid them by denying their existence? Self-honesty can be very challenging. However, once it is developed, it is also very freeing. Untold secrets, denial, resistance, and all white knuckling melt away.

Questions To Facilitate Your Inner Exploration

1. Go over your answers to the questions presented to you so far in this book. Can you see areas where it was difficult to be completely honest with yourself?

2. Reflect on and describe those areas of your life.

Your Relationship with the Holding Space

If you don't have a healthy relationship with what lies within you, it can be hard to take a look at yourself and see what lies below the surface. For instance, what you may have been doing to feel comfortable with yourself is white knuckling on to an identity of who you think you are.

This prevents you from resting into your inner holding space.

It is sometimes taught that people are inherently bad and behave sinfully when they succumb to their inherent nature. This is only true if the physiology is stressed. If the physiology is free from stress, the inherent behavior is spontaneously positive and life-affirming. When we don't understand this, we usually strive to be good by piling up more and more identities in an attempt to align with something positive that lies outside of ourselves. That creates even more stress, which leads to disease and psychological ill health.

So the path to right action is through the purification of the physiology, not through conformity to any set of psychological, puritanical, or other standards; however, well-intentioned they may be. Social parameters, cultural guidelines, educational guidelines, role models, and our idealized notions of how we think we will be when we're "self-improved" can distract us from the path to inherent right action.

Band-Aid Therapy

Band-Aid therapy is the structuring of the surface to look as acceptable as possible independently from what lies underneath. It is like sweeping the dust under the rug.

All too often we approach our psychotherapy as Band-Aid therapy. We identify something we don't like about ourselves and try to stop doing it. At times, it's quite appropriate, but we must realize that it is not the healing. For example, if you decide you get angry too often and learn to suppress your anger, that can be a good thing. However, the stress is still there in your physiology. No healing has taken place. Band-Aid therapy is best used as a quick fix to keep your unhealthy tendencies in check while you continue with your inner exploration. The inner exploration facilitates the self-correcting mechanism that brings about the true healing.

Other Band-Aids we acquire are moral codes, guidelines, and rules. These external overlays that we conform to are just like training wheels on a bicycle. They are not going make you mentally healthy, but they can help you along the way until you can ride the two-wheel bicycle of life by yourself. Training wheels are only needed because we have lost touch with our own inner wisdom and common sense. When you become a responsible, healthy, and mentally stable individual, you write the guidelines with your life. Everyday situations are usually too complex for any set of rules to address. To make proper decisions, we need to refer to the vessel that holds the understanding of life: the resting place inside. That is the place that is already wise, has always been wise, and will always be wise.

The Experiment Called Your Life

At any given moment, you can only do your best with life's situations. You can't always know what the best or appropriate action is. You work at developing a viable response, and at some point you just have to take your best shot. Then you see what comes back from your environment. Based upon what comes back, you come to further conclusions, work with them, and develop another response. If you wait until you absolutely know what to do before you do something, you'll never do anything. All you can ever do is take your best shot. So in that sense, there's no such thing as a mistake. Life is a big exploration. You try one thing, see what happens, and based on that you make another call. So there are no mistakes. Life is just a big experiment.

Question: If you don't really know and just stumble along, how do you make progress in your life?

Progress in life is the result of what you do with those experiences. It's a result of what you do with what comes back. That brings up the concept of "relationship with" that affects not only decision-making, but also everything else that goes on in your life.

What's your relationship with what goes on inside your head? Cultivating a healthy relationship with it is critical. We are often taught by our society to be cruel in our relationships with ourselves, and with what goes on between our ears. We judge it and we judge our judgments of it. We tell ourselves we've got a problem. We are messed up. We are nuts. Or we are just stumbling along. It's a very unhealthy relationship with the self. It gives no space.

Actually, giving yourself space is about being in that

resting place inside. Cultivating the physiological state spontaneously gives you psychological space.

Feeling Your Way

The resting space can almost sound like a contradiction. It's a state of resting into your being but simultaneously being alert and dynamic. It is a state of behaving "properly," yet not being cramped by your behavior. To understand how that could be comes from understanding the nature of life. You're never going to be able to fathom everything in life with the intellect and come to the right conclusion. Feelings lie deeper than intellect. We feel our way through life. We don't think our way through life.

You need to give yourself the space to feel your way through life because feelings are the basis of reason. Reason is, in turn, the basis of thoughts. Feelings should not be interpreted as the abandonment of logic. Feelings are the underlying basis of logic. This logic is not a collection of circular intellectual loops but is connected to the depth and breath of your being.

If there is a lot of stress in your physiology, what you're feeling is the stress. Where there is stress there is identity. Where there is identity there is limitation. Where there is limitation there is a limited "relationship with," which ultimately leads to a blind alley and creates a double bind. Double binds are why I sometimes describe inner work as trying to punch your way out of a bag. It sometimes feels like you can't get any leverage. When you get yourself all tied up in a knot with these double binds, the way to work with it is to just be easy with it. Just give it space, get out of the way, and feel your way. In other words, don't let your stress get in the way. Just be easy with it and give it space.

Your Finest Feelings

When your psychophysiology is healthy, it is refined. The emotions that well up in your being are integrated with and a reflection of your finest feelings. That integration enables you to live your life wisely. You then experience the depth of your being through the subtle, exquisite, sublime sensing of your inner purity. Your thoughts, feelings, and longings are inspired by those fine feelings. When there is stress in the physiology, the waves of emotion have lost their connection to the finest feelings at the depth of your being. What lies at the depth of every individual is a beautiful angelic soul.

Chapter 4

Day Four:
Mastering Your Inner Process

When things become more subtle and complex, keeping your balance becomes more difficult. The instinct is to grab on to an old identity and hang on for dear life. In Day Four we're going to discuss some subtle and complex topics. Just keep your balance, and do your inner exploration. This will cultivate within you a more refined relationship not only with your self, but also with what you have learned these past few days. That will prepare you to take this knowledge with you when you leave, and keep it lively in your daily life. If you do that, your life will become a powerful catalyst to your self-discovery.

Cultivating a Healthy Sense of Self

We need to understand that mental health is about having a healthy relationship with different paradigms. There is no "ice cream cone in the sky" perspective that is going to answer all your questions or make you a whole person. You have to cultivate a certain level of flexibility to move from one perspective to another and to see which serves life the best in any given moment. Sometimes logic works and other times feelings work. We do not find our stability by holding onto one or the other. We find our stability by resting into that deeper place inside characterized by what I call a "sense of self."

As a culture, we don't have any understanding of how to develop that sense of self. Even in the field of psychology, there is very little understanding of the physiological state that truly stabilizes our lives. Yet, it is fundamentally important. From this fundamental sense of self, we rest into our own innate beauty and exquisiteness. If we feel we have to claim our own exquisiteness, that means we don't have it.

Question: Can we attain this state of psychological health through our will power?

It is not an attitude; it's a physiological state. So it is not something you can will. It is not something you can decide to do. You can't walk out the door and say, "Okay, now I'm going to rest into myself."

Question: Now that I see what I've been doing that is unhealthy, what do I do about it?

The response can always be the same. You are doing something about it. This is the doing. The doing is the exploration. You are turning over the stones on the beach of your own inner landscape right now just by talking about it. What is under this stone in the contour of your inner landscape? What's behind that rock? This is the exploration, the tilling of the soil. Anything we try then to do about it amounts to a Band-Aid: "Oh, I see I was this way, and so now I will start being that way."

Your Personality

Your personality is a very superficial level of your being. Some people have personalities that cause them to get angry often. Other people have personalities that cause them to be sweet and loving. You take a huge step forward in your understanding of life and your ability to do your own inner exploration responsibly when you realize that your personality doesn't really matter. It's your relationship with your personality that matters.

Your Relationship With Power

I think any society that makes a man wear a tie and a woman wear pantyhose and high heels must be a rather cruel society. I was walking around Manhattan the other day and saw a woman in high heels running after the bus. As I watched her, I realized she was having difficulty running. It was horrible to watch. I thought, "Oh my God, it seems so unnatural." Putting a woman in high heels seemed, at that moment, to be a means of taking away her power. Similarly, putting a necktie around a man's throat also takes away his power.

I thought of the ancient Chinese practice of binding feet. It is all about vulnerability, but vulnerability in a twisted sense. Our relationship with vulnerability can be healthy or unhealthy. When does vulnerability, an exquisite quality, cease to be vulnerability? When does it become weakness? When does it become disempowering? There are aspects of the healthy male and female principle that are profoundly and beautifully vulnerable. We can simultaneously be profoundly vulnerable and powerful.

Our culture has lost touch with what it means to have power, particularly for a woman. It doesn't mean that she has to burn her bras and wear army boots. It doesn't mean she has to act like a man and go toe to toe with a man in the arena of manliness. That's a gross misunderstanding of the power inherent to the feminine aspect.

Question: I think we equate the word power with the idea of being masculine. As a woman, when I go to family get-togethers, I always feel looked down upon somehow.

An important part of your inner exploration is to look at your relationship with the notion of power. The most powerful thing you bring into any relationship is yourself. It's about the degree to which you are resting into your self, not as a badge you are wearing or your armoring. That's the true power of the feminine principle, as well as the masculine.

Consider Leonardo Da Vinci's *Mona Lisa*. Every time I look at that painting, I wonder what she was thinking and what she knew that Da Vinci did not know. That subtle, yet overpowering, look in her eyes and the smile on her lips are very powerful illustrations of the feminine principle. The male principle can bring a person to his knees with a baseball bat. The feminine principle can bring a person to his knees with a glance.

Questions To Facilitate Your Inner Exploration

1. What does it mean to you for a man to be in his power?

2. What does it mean to you for a woman to be in her power?

3. What is your relationship with your power? Does your power scare you? Do you think your relationship with your power is healthy? Unhealthy? Elaborate.

4. Think of some powerful people that you feel have an unhealthy relationship with their power. Select some men and some women. Describe your thoughts and feelings about them.

5. Repeat #4 for powerful people you feel have a healthy relationship with their power.

6. Now consider people you know who do not seem to be very powerful in their lives. Please discuss.

Inner Space

Sometimes our mind starts going around and around, jumping from one perspective to another. What is going on in our heads seems to be a big unending buzz of conflicting notions.

Question: Yes, it gets cluttered in there sometimes.

When you really get in your mind and start picking things apart, eventually there can be no space left for you to rest. Anytime you apply any of the notions I've presented, like motivation, you can end up chasing yourself around in circles and tying yourself up in a knot with it. It's important to just take a look at how it is you tie yourself up in knots. Notice that this is one way you don't give yourself any inner space.

My wife and I saw the movie "Meet Joe Black." One thing I liked about Bill Perish, the character played by Anthony Hopkins, was the way he related to people: he gave them space. When he asked a question, he was okay with somebody sidestepping it. His attitude was, "Well, these things just have a way of sorting themselves out." We need to learn to do that with ourselves. We need to learn to give ourselves some space inside of our own psyche. To give space to ourselves and others is a wonderful gift. It is beautiful when someone gives you that sort of space in a relationship or in a family. It doesn't necessarily mean you don't call for long periods of time. What it means is when you're in someone's presence, conversing with and relating to that person, you give that person some space to be, to feel, and to think.

Question: Could you say giving space is just allowing it to be the way it is?

You could say it that way. Giving space also has to do with knowing that if your relationship with your habits is easy, you'll start to move beyond them.

Question: Can this apply to not being easy with time?

Sure. Not being easy with time can strip you of your space. You never have time for yourself. You rush around and judge yourself by whether or not you're on time. Does that mean part of giving yourself space is being late? No. There are people that don't give themselves any space around time that are never on time. There are people that give themselves plenty of space around time that are always on time. But the point here is to simply explore your relationship with your own inner space. The awareness is the healing. If you just explore it, it will self-correct. If you try to do it right, it just becomes one more thing you don't give yourself any space around.

Question: So it's okay to have idiosyncrasies?

We could say it's about having a healthy relationship with your idiosyncrasies.

Question: So effort can almost make things worse?

If you try to push out aspects of yourself, they will stay with you longer. You, in effect, just drive them deeper.

Perhaps they are swept under the rug, but they are still there.

Question: Does this apply to addictions?

If you try to sweep aspects of yourself under the rug, your relationship with them can become a form of neurosis; an obsessive, self-punitive, and self-destructive kind of a relationship. Giving them space doesn't mean not taking them seriously and exerting effort. Giving space is like an internal kindness.

Questions To Facilitate Your Inner Exploration

1. Think of a problem that has been a source of confusion to you, something that has caused your mind to go back and forth incessantly from one viewpoint to the next. Remember each of these viewpoints.

2. Now just make the choice to be easy with the inner chatter around the whole situation. Give it space. Know that these things have a way of working themselves out.

Good, Evil, and the Finest Feeling Level

Your notion of good and evil is a major player in you inner psychodynamic structure. We all have little voices whispering in our ear. In the arena of modern psychology, these voices are collectively called the superego, your conscience.

Wise individuals throughout history looked out at the world and observed the behavior of people. They saw some behaviors supported life and other behaviors compromised the health of the culture. These very well intended and wise individuals came up with doctrines, "If you do this, you're good. If you do that, you're bad." People made creeds out of these notions regarding good and evil. It is really that simple.

Those creeds came from the fine feeling level of wise individuals. So the origin of those doctrines was very much an in/out process. Striving to align with the creeds is an out/in endeavor. We can never access our wisdom through an out/in alignment with a set of codes of conduct.

These codes need to be held, but held wisely. They are precious knowledge passed down throughout the ages. They need to be respected. But if, in the respecting of them, you end up losing connection to your own deeper self, the codes have begun to compromise you. So your relationship with them too must be healthy.

The codes of conduct are valuable if we use them to further facilitate our ability to touch into that place inside and function from there. They're training wheels. Training wheels meet their fulfillment when they are no longer needed by the bicyclist.

So wisdom regarding good and evil is not held in any set of doctrines. It is held in the finest feelings of healthy people, the people who have loosened their white-knuckled grip on their identities, even their identities with what they have been told makes them good!

Question: So what is evil?

Evil is the state of an agitated psychophysiology. It is the lack of psychodynamic integration. It's the lack of ability to access and function from inner wisdom. What lies at the basis of every individual's being is pure good. There is no such thing as absolute evil. The Evil Sorcerer archetype is just somebody who has lost his connection with his inner purity.

100 Percent Responsibility

If you are in conflict with another person it is often valuable to view the conflict as if you are 100 percent responsible for the difficulty. Blaming the other person may interfere with the exploration of aspects of your inner psyche that need healing. You can gain insights into your own inner landscape by considering yourself 100 percent responsible for that conflict. Thus, the healthiest relationship to have with the notion of 100 percent responsibilities is to view it as a tool that can sometimes facilitate your inner exploration. Having a healthy relationship with any psychodynamic perspective means that you can freely pick the perspective up and lay it back down based on what best serves your inner exploration at that moment.

Questions To Facilitate Your Inner Exploration

1. Think of a conflict you have had with someone recent-
    ly. Now reexamine that conflict from the perspective
    that you were 100 percent responsible for its creation.
    How did you create it? What could you have done dif-
    ferently?

2. How did the perspective of "100 percent responsibili-
    ty" facilitate your inner exploration? Did you gain any
    insights into your psychodynamic landscape?

3. Repeat this process with other difficult situations or
    predicaments in your life.

Fulfillment of Your Inner Longing

This world is a world of longing. It's a world of wanting. Longing is the nature of life. Where we feel separation, we long to become whole. We tend to look to the
surface of our lives to fulfill that wanting. We find plenty
of things on the surface we would like to come together
with: money, nice clothes, friends—you create your own
list. Yet there are plenty of stories about people who, after
fulfilling these longings, are still miserable.

It is natural and healthy to want on the surface level of
life. But the basis of the longing is not on the surface of
life; it's deeper. The basis is a wanting to feel whole, a
wanting to be full. And that will never be filled from
out/in. That will never be filled by making the surface of

your life conform to your idealized vision.

Fulfillment is a physiological state. Our deepest longing is the longing for a state of mental health, of physiological integration, a fullness of our own being. We get into difficulties when we attempt to quench our deepest longing by feeding the surface. It is not that we need to cease to try to feed personality wants. Feeding the personality wants is normal and healthy. But when we think that doing so will quench the deeper longing, we're sadly mistaken.

Plenty of people have invested their life into fulfilling their surface wants and been successful. They don't want to look any deeper. They're afraid to look at the depth of their own being because part of them knows that they are not full. A part of them knows that inside they are really not happy. They'd rather be in denial of it. But it always catches up with them. You can only live in denial so long.

So we do well to explore our longing. We explore it by feeling it and reflecting on it. What's its nature? How does it feel inside? This exploration is another gateway to mental health. People who explore their longing with self-honesty will see that what they want is to feel full inside. They want to feel inner satisfaction and contentment. They want the deepest and most profound sense of the self. It's not the thought of self or an image of self. It's a sense of self deep in their being that resonates at the depth of the physiology, purrs like a kitten, and hums like the idle of a well-tuned car. This is the underlying deepest longing for all individuals and the source of true self-esteem.

Your Notion of a Higher Self

The "higher self" is another notion you can employ to facilitate your inner exploration. But your relationship with that notion is important too. The higher self is sometimes considered to be your true identity. It is said to be your "positive attributes," including your love, nobility, truth, goodness, serenity, righteousness, beauty, and so on. Your notion of the higher self is very much a product of your conditioning. It is what you think it means to be completely self-improved. The notion of the higher self is usually similar to a Hollywood movie's melodramatic version of Jesus.

It is a valuable exercise to explore your notions of the higher self. Where did those notions come from? Your parents? Church? Teachers? How might they be inconsistent with your personality? What will you really be like when you have a healthy psychophysiology? How might your notions of higher self set you up for a life of low self-esteem and failure? Could you ever live up to them? How might those notions set you up for a life of judgment, not only of yourself, but also of others? Could they ever live up to those notions? For example, when you notice that someone is being judgmental, you may judge their judgement as their inability to live up to your notion of their higher self!

When you attempt to conform to your notion of

higher self, you abandon who you truly are to reach for an idealized notion, a vision in the sky. Your true self, after the stresses and strains become purified out from your psychophysiology, is something that lies beyond the access of an out/in approach. It is simplistic to believe that you can possibly know what you will be like when the stresses and strains are out of your system. The only way you can know it is to be it.

In reality, when the stresses and strains are freed from your physiology you probably won't look at all like what you and others may envision your higher self to be. You will still get angry and sad. You will still have conflicts and feel hurt. As you become more and more psychodynamically healthy, your personality does not need to change. You will still be very human! Psychological health is not about personality modification. Yet the notion of higher self is all about personality. It's a bogus and cruel barometer to gauge yourself by.

Questions To Facilitate Your Inner Exploration

1. What has been your notion of your higher (or perhaps you would prefer the term "idealized") self?

2. Where did this notion come from? Your mother? Your father? A spiritual teacher? School?

3. What did you do with that notion, subconsciously, before you knew the term, "higher self"?

4. What did your notion, in turn, do to you? Set you up
   with a fantasy for a lifetime goal? Make you judgmental of yourself and others? Divert your efforts in an
   erroneous direction?

5. What insights can you gain into your psychodynamic
   landscape as you explore your relationship with your
   notions of your higher self?

6. How have your attempts to live up to or claim your
   higher self actually interfered with you development?

7. How is your notion of your higher self different from
   what you have learned in this book about what it is like
   to be psychologically healthy?

8. How can the notion of higher self become the inspiration for a lifetime of Band-Aid therapy?

Your Notion of a Lower Self

Your "lower self" is considered to be the source of
your negative attitudes toward yourself or other people. It
gives rise to your desire to remain separate from your
deeper self and from other people.

If you are familiar with the notions of higher self and
lower self, it is likely that you categorize the attributes that
you like about yourself as coming from the higher self and
the attributes that you dislike about yourself as coming
from the lower self. Such notions are usually based more
on conditioning than inner truth. There are attributes of

your behavior, when its functioning in a mentally healthy manner, that you may currently categorize as lower self and want to eliminate from your personality. For example, every time you get angry, have a negative feeling, or are hurtful to anybody you may think: "Oh, chalk that one up to my lower self."

The notions of higher and lower self can be valuable tools to assist your inner exploration. But if you are not careful, they can compel you to live up to your conditioned identities instead of discovering your deeper inner nature and truth.

The model is not what is important. If you look at it closely, the model of higher/lower self is a fantasy. Yet exploring your relationship with that fantasy can be a valuable tool to facilitate your self discovery.

Perhaps it would be more accurate to define lower self as that aspect of yourself that compromises life. Consider, then, that clinging on to the notion of your higher self has its basis in your lower self. Where you cling, you are lost to an identity. Identity compromises life.

Questions To Facilitate Your Inner Exploration

1. What has been your notion of your lower self?

2. Where did those notions come from? Your mother? Your father? Church? School?

3. What did you do with that notion, subconsciously, before you knew the term, "lower self"?

4. What, in turn, did it do to you? How did it affect your life? Your relationships? Your health? Other aspects of your life?

5. What insights can you gain into your psychodynamic landscape as you explore your relationship with your notions of your lower self?

6. How have your attempts to overcome your lower self actually interfered with you development? Have they led to Band-Aid therapy? Misdirected efforts?

7. How has your relationship with your notion of your lower self changed from what you have learned in this book about what it is like to be psychologically healthy?

Your Notion of the Mask

The "mask" is said to be your superficial identity or how you try to present yourself to the world. It is who you think you are supposed to be in daily life. It is how you change the spontaneity of your being to make yourself appear to be okay. In some circles it has a negative connotation associated with it: "If you really have it together, you'll be in your higher self all the time. When you're in your mask you are being phony." That's not necessarily true. It is important not only to have a mask but also to have a healthy relationship with it. There are things that are appropriate, respect social convention, and ease the process of interfacing with other people. When you are functioning from a healthy psychophysiology, you'll still honor and conform to that sort of thing. Being psychologically healthy does not mean free-flowing impulsiveness every moment. There will still be times when you need to practice some restraint. That restraint becomes an exquisite thing. It becomes qualities that we may describe as dignity, respect, and proper behavior. It is only when we lose our self to our mask that it takes on an unhealthy value.

Once again, "relationship with" makes all the difference. How has your relationship with the mask been healthy? How has it been unhealthy? When does your attempt to behave properly become self-compromising? So when our relationship with the mask is healthy, the mask is actually quite a beautiful thing. It is something we offer to other people out of respect for them and for the community. Just basic respect, embraced through the vehicle of the mask, is a very important part of healthy relationships. A healthy mask is an aspect of a healthy mind. To long for a time when you will never "be in your mask" is reaching for a mirage, a delusion.

The following questions will illustrate how the notion of your mask can be a valuable tool to facilitate your inner exploration.

Questions To Facilitate Your Inner Exploration

1. What is your mask like?

2. What experiences in your life created you mask? With

your mother? Your father? Church? School? Where else?

3. What did you do with that, subconsciously, before you learned about the notion of mask?

4. What, in turn, did that do to you? How did it affect your life? Your relationships? Other aspects of your life?

5. How has your relationship with your mask compromised you? How can it serve you?

6. How has your relationship with your mask been healthy? How has it been unhealthy?

7. What insights can you gain into your psychodynamic landscape as you explore your relationship with your notions of your mask self?

7. How have your attempts to live up to your mask self interfered with you development? How have they assisted it?

8. Think of people you may know who you feel have unhealthy relationships with their masks. Describe the relationship and explain why it is unhealthy.

9. Think of people who have healthy relationships with their masks. Describe and explain.

10. How may your relationship with your mask change based upon what you have learned in this book about psychological health?

The Reason, Will, Emotion Model

Some people are predominantly reason-oriented. They think and reason their way through life.

Some people are predominantly emotion-oriented. First and foremost, they want an emotional connection. They want to feel you. What is important to them is how they feel when they experience others. For example, they might feel hurt or full. Whatever they feel is what they consider to be important.

Other people are predominantly will-oriented. They have their idea of what they want to attain and ramrod their way through life. They find their fulfillment and success in life by how well they can make things happen according to their will. It is not that they are ill-intended. They may simply feel that they know best.

The reason, will, and emotion model is often poorly applied. People decide which one they predominantly are and try to suppress it while developing the other two more. The idea is that by doing so they will come more into balance. For example, someone may conclude, "Oh well, gee, I'm predominantly will. I do reason a lot though to bring forth my will, so I have to become more emotional. I have to get more into my emotions." Another person might decide, "I'm predominantly emotion, so I need a little more reason and will to balance that out." That is not the proper use of this model. In fact, that's a good example of turning an understanding into an identity overlay. It's like trying to turn apples into oranges and turning trees into two-by-fours. It's tantamount to turning yourself into a psychodynamic Barbie or Ken doll.

You are what you are. Some people are more reason-oriented. Others are more will-oriented. Still others are more emotion-oriented. That doesn't need to change. It's just your personality.

But the value of the reason, will, and emotion model is that it can be used as an "in" to facilitate an exploration of your inner landscape so the self-correcting mechanism can do its work. So in a healthy relationship with this model, we spend a little time reflecting: "Do I predominantly use reason, will, or emotion? How does my reason interact with my will and my emotion? What is my relationship with reason, with will, and with emotions? How does my inner landscape operate in terms of that model?"

This model can be a very powerful gateway to your psychodynamic exploration. The exploration yields its fruit naturally.

Questions To Facilitate Your Inner Exploration

1. Are you predominantly reason-oriented, will-oriented, or emotion-oriented?

2. What is the relationship between your reason, will, and emotion? Do they communicate and work well with each other? Does one judge the others? Does one hide behind the others?

3. Are you more comfortable with one than the others?

Can you relate this to your childhood experiences?

4. From the perspective of this model, do you think your friends or loved ones would see you the way you see yourself? Elaborate.

5. Reflect upon people you know in the light of the questions above.

Preverbal Issues

For adults, every experience is accompanied by words, verbal conceptualizations, and rationales dancing around in their heads. In contrast, when you were a newborn, what you experienced was what you felt. During the first several months of your life, you did not conceptualize those experiences into words because you had no words.

As an infant, before you were able to speak, you experienced things in an intangible, abstract way. If these experiences imposed stress on your psychophysiology, you may find them very difficult to relate to as an adult. Although the stresses entered as intangible abstractions, you are naturally inclined to face them through tangible verbal pathways. That is simply the way your adult mind has learned to function. But when you go back into that time, you enter an inner space of no words. For that reason, stresses based on preverbal trauma can be difficult to work with as an adult.

Question: So how do we know how to approach a problem?

If you're having problems accessing some aspect of what's going on within your psyche through inner exploration, then try another way. One way is through herbs. There is a myriad of other ways. Proper meditation purifies psychophysiological stress. Through meditation, you never need to identify beliefs. They just clear as the stress clears.

Question: Can a psychotherapist help?

There's certainly a role for therapists; they can support and facilitate the exploration. If there is an area that we keep missing or that we're in denial of, a gentle suggestion like, "Hey, let's take a look over here," can be very helpful. Also just the idea that they're with you can be comforting. However, you must choose who you work with carefully. There are many different psychotherapeutic, self-help, and spiritual approaches. Some can be harmful.

Potential Pitfalls in Your Personal Process

Question: Where do most people who do their personal process get stuck?

The biggest potential pitfall in your own inner exploration is aligning with paradigms or approaches to your personal process that are not consistent with the nature of the human psyche and how it normalizes. That can be a challenge because this field is bombarded with out/in approaches. There are many new self-help books coming out every month. If you read self-help books, you would do well to view them in the context of what you've learned here. Now, please take note: This is easier said than done. It's very easy to lose touch with the fundamentals and get swept away. This knowledge is deceptively subtle and elusive.

Many people who have returned to attend another one of my classes say, "When I sit here and listen to you talk, what you say makes perfect sense. But when I go out into the world, it is a challenge sometimes to even remember what you said."

That is because the in/out approach is not common. Most people approach the world from out to in. That's what we have become accustomed to. The out/in approach is a habit. Anyone who has tried to lose weight knows how hard it can be to break habits. So when you see a book called *Twenty Steps to a Better You*, or *Sixty Days to Enlightenment*, remember that they are appealing because that type of thinking has been programmed into the mass psyche. Because the out/in approach is a habit, it requires some attention to prevent the understanding I've presented here from being converted in your mind into a white-knuckled out/in approach. So beware. I understand the longing to grab on to something that might move you forward, but so many things we do to move forward are ultimately things that end up holding us back. So choose, but choose wisely. Be discriminating. Be judgmental. Quick fix, simplistic, out/in understandings are the biggest pitfall to your process. That's the place where most people get lost.

Also, when you hear of the notion of self-improve-ment, don't forget that it's not about self-improvement. I like an expression that has been attributed to different people: "If you spend your whole life working on your self-improvement, all you'll have to show for it at the end your life is an improved self." What we're talking about here is the difference between personality modification and resting into your own true nature. Self-improvement generally falls into the category of personality modifica-tion. That's not the source of true mental health.

Question: There is no one in my home town who understands these ideas: in/out, relationship with, identity, sense of self, and so on. But I want to have community, to have people I can dis-cuss my personal process with.

When we go to a therapist, teacher, or study group, we have to pass much of what they're saying and doing through the filter of this understanding, which can be dif-ficult. But we still go because the thirst for community can be very powerful.

That thirst can become destructive when we compro-mise the subtlety of what we know to go along with a mainstream attitude or behavioral pattern. That com-monly takes the form of, "Well, they are really saying the same thing. The difference is just semantics." The most precious understandings of life have been lost to seman-tics. It gets lost in the translation, so to speak. So look to see how the things you are exposed to are different from what you have learned here, not how they are the same.

Question: How does one go about finding a reliable therapist or teacher?

Feel, listen, think, reflect, and ponder. After the test of time, decide whom you would like to work with. Someone once asked for advice on a very important problem. He was told, "Just follow your heart." I say, "No, don't just follow your heart. Think, feel, reflect, ponder, contemplate, take your time, and give yourself space with it." This is someone you're entrusting as facilitator of your own personal process. The fabric is too fine, too precious. The distortions and distractions can sweep you away at great cost to your psychophysiological health. The therapist's may sound similar to the words here, but the knowledge of life is subtle. The difference that makes all the difference lies in the subtlety of that distinction.

Question: What other things do you think are of value?

For one, sleep! I see many people running around to therapists, herbalists, and healers who I feel would be better to just get some more rest. Also, bodywork. A good deep tissue massage can do a tremendous amount. Invest time into your psychological health but use that time wisely.

Conclusion

Knowing about something is very different from embodying it. You can intellectually know that to play a piano, your hands and fingers must perform precise movements in relation to the keys. But that does not mean you can play a piano. Likewise, intellectually understanding psychodynamic health is just the beginning. Applying what you have learned here in an ongoing manner is what is important. You attain and then maintain your psychodynamic health by relating to yourself and others in a manner consistent with this knowledge. As you progress, this process becomes easier. This understanding becomes increasingly self-evident and spontaneous. Why? Because it is consistent with your true nature.

As the sweetness of your inner being shines forth into your life, your own self-love becomes a beacon light for others. Your cup, full and overflowing, nourishes and supports the lives of those around you. When the tree of your inner life is filled with the fruit of your being, the branches of your soul just naturally bow down and touch the earth in humility. Then you are truly wise, happy, self assured, and abundant. Then you are truly free.

Selected Readings

Baker, Elsworth. *Man in the Trap*. New York: Colliers Books (1980).

Boadella, David. *Wilhelm Reich: The Evolution of His Works*. Chicago: Henry Regnery Company (1973).

Cornsweet, David. *The Reichian Legacy*. San Diego: International College (1983).

Johnson, Robert. *Inner Work*. San Francisco: Harper (1989).

Lowen, Alexander. *The Language of the Body*. New York: Macmillan Publishing Co. (1958).

Bioenergetics (1975).

Pierrakos, John C. *Core Energetics*. Mendocino: Life Rhythm Publication (1987).

Reich, Wilhelm. *The Function of the Orgasm*. New York: Farrar, Strauss and Giroux, Inc. (1961).

Rogers, Carl. *A Way of Being*. Boston: Houghton Mifflin (1980).

Rogers, Carl. *On Becoming a Person*. Boston: Houghton Mifflin (1995).

Winnicott, D.W. *Family and Individual Development*. Routledge (1996).

Freud, Sigmund. *Interpretations of Dreams*. Mass Market Paperback (1983).

Satir, Virginia. *New Peoplemaking*. Science and Behavior Books, 2nd Edition (1988)

Jung, Carl. *Man and His Symbols*. Doubleday, 2nd Edition(1969)

Perls, Fritz. *In and Out of the Garbage Pail*. Gestalt Journal Printing, Reprint Edition (1992)

About the Author

Dr. Michael Mamas was an honors student in physics and mathematics. He has a doctorate in veterinary medicine and a Masters degree in business administration, and is an Ordained Minister. He lived in a monastery for nine years and has been doing counseling work for nearly thirty years. Dr. Mamas lives in Asheville, NC, with his wife Tanja and daughter Jaya.

After closing his private practice in 1994, he started lecturing around the country and offering *The Surya Program*™, an ongoing series of intensive classes for personal development and training in *Transgradient Healing*™ and *Transgradient Counseling*™. As a leader in health care, Dr. Mamas has an extensive knowledge of herbal and other health care modalities. Products based upon his knowledge are made available to the public in the catalog, *Surya Essentials*™.

For more information on *The Surya Program*, or for a schedule of lectures with locations and class times, please call 1-888-432-5888, or visit Dr. Mamas's website at www.DrMamas.com.

The Surya Program

D r. Mamas offers a series of long weekend classes called The Surya Program™ leading to certification in Transgradient Healing and Transgradient Counseling. This unique program gives participants the opportunity to explore and work with the principles Dr. Mamas speaks about in this book. The curriculum is designed for students who are interested in facilitating the healing of others as a profession as well as for those who are interested solely in their own personal growth. The Surya Program is attended by people of all walks of life from homemakers to health professionals, librarians to lawyers. It is accredited for continuing education for psychotherapists (MFCC and LCSW) and nurses.

Classes are held in Asheville, NC, and the San Francisco Bay Area. The program is designed in such a way that students from around the world are able to attend, fitting the program in with their ongoing professional and family commitments. Surya One, the six-day introductory class, is offered in various cities throughout the nation.

If you are interested in attending the program or would like to receive a brochure please contact:

The Surya Program
PO Box 8051
Asheville, NC 28814
888-432-5888
surya@dr.mamas.com
www.DrMamas.com

To order additional copies of:

How To Be
Your Own Best Psychotherapist

Book: $18.95 • Shipping/Handling: $4.95
or for copies of other books by Dr. Michael Mamas

Contact: SEH, Inc.
P.O. Box 8051
Asheville, NC 28814

E-mail: books@drmamas.com
Fax: 828-236-0655
Phone: 1-800-432-5888